Pacific Book Review

helping authors succeed!

Title: Covered By Grace
Author: Mary Berry
Genre: Religion & Spirituality
Reviewed by: Aly Avina

Pacific Book Review

Every now and then, a book comes along that makes you think and ponder over your own life and the decisions you've made. t is a book which not only helps you reflect upon your life but helps you discover ways to make it more meaningful than before. That is precisely what you can expect from this book, *Covered By Grace*" by author Mary Berry. It is an in-depth look into faith and hope, after feeling as though all is lost. By definition, "Grace" is "biblically defined as the unmerited, unearned, and undeserved favor and/or blessings from God" which is explained to the audience early on in this book. This is a helpful descriptor particularly for those who may not be as familiar with religion and Christian values. Berry makes sure to deliver on explanations that will help those who are unfamiliar with Christian terminology better understand her story and redemption.

All throughout this book, we are treated with meaningful scriptures which coincide with the part of the story she is currently touching on. It helps engage the audience and vividly brings them to an understanding of what it is which could help them in their own journey of forgiveness for past sins. Many of the book's core values in which Berry touches on are applicable to anyone going through a hardship, particularly one that was caused by their own doing. Berry lets go of all her fears of sharing her own sins and connects with her audience by recounting her own journey of guilt and shame until the day she felt she was forgiven after repenting for said sins. God's grace is what helped her move on from the past into a life of deeper meaning and faith in her faith in God and religion.

For those of you who may not be religious, don't let that deter you from a book such as this. It has many great life lessons that can apply to most people's lives in one way or another. Furthermore, for those who easily relate to this book due to the religious nature of it, it will be a great read which will leave you wanting to accept your past sins, repent, and eventually strengthen your own relationship with God. It is a beautifully written novel that touches on many important subjects, including forgiving yourself after years of guilt and shame have weighed on you. This is one you won't want to miss, so be sure to pick up your copy of *Covered By Grace* by Mary Berry today!

COVERED BY GRACE

May God's grace
cover you in all
your coming and going
in the Lord.
Love ya —
MaryAnn Berry

MARY BERRY

Quotations and paraphrases from Katie Souza Ministries, www.expectedendministries.org. Used by permission.

Quotations and paraphrases from Derek Prince International, INC. www.derekprince.org. Used by permission.

Printed in the United States of America.

Library of Congress Control Number: 2019918769

ISBN   Paperback   978-1-64361-963-7
              eBook   978-1-64361-964-4

Westwood Books Publishing LLC
11416 SW Aventino Drive
Port Saint Lucie, FL 34987

www.westwoodbookspublishing.com

ENDORSEMENTS

"Powerful, edifying, equipping and educating! *Covered by Grace* creates a desire for inward reflection and deeper, broader in-depth study of God's love and The Power of His Grace! It is a great addition to any library."

Connections Pastor, Brian Ulch,
Trinity Lighthouse Church, Denison, TX

"*Covered by Grace* is a powerful testimony of Mary Ann Berry's journey of becoming daringly transparent and exposing her own secret sin. It is a story of how she traded shame, sorrow, and remorse for peace, love, and joy. Intertwined in her personal story is one of the most Biblical definitions of what God's true grace really is."

Senior Pastor, Raymond England,
Trinity Lighthouse Church, Denison, TX

Mary Berry

"What a courageous way to describe the amazing depth of God's grace. I applaud your transparency… few people are daring enough to describe themselves with such rawness and honesty. Your candor was refreshing. Your book provides excellent teaching on the scandalous and reckless power of God's grace. I believe lives will be changed by this freeing grace you have so vividly described."

Executive Pastor, Gwen England,
Trinity Lighthouse Church, Denison, TX

"In her second book, *Covered By Grace,* Mary opens her heart to God's forgiving grace for past failure. She includes scriptural principles, insights, and the theology of receiving God's total cleansing. I would recommend this book to those who need a touch of in depth understanding of how His grace covers all of our short-comings."

Harriett Nix - Pastor's wife, Sunday school Bible teacher,
and retired schoolteacher, Sherman, TX

DEDICATION

To all Christians who have stubbed their toe, fallen,
skinned their knees, elbows, and face, and have
struggled to run again on that narrow rocky road.
The Lord cries out,
"Receive My *grace!*"
"Get up; get going; be watchful, for there is much work to be done!"
"All my children are needed in the fields white with harvest."

CONTENTS

PREFACE

$\mathscr{C}$OVERED BY *GRACE* IS penned initially from the hand of a rebellious writer, adamantly declaring, "No, Lord," refusing to consider, even in the slightest degree, the assignment. As days gave way to months and months gave way to years, this reluctant writer was cocooned in transformation. Being exhausted from constant battle, this author ultimately surrendered wholly becoming the Lord's servant, regardless of personal preferences.

The Lord says, "Hold your head up high above the sting of perceived shame, guilt, regret, and remorse, from even what you consider abhorrent. I am with you always." Covered by *Grace* is a personal account of transformation through our Lord's miraculous, merciful, and unrelenting love. The Lord desires that none should perish, but that all come to a knowledge of the truth (1 Timothy 2:4; 2 Peter 3:9).

Covered by *Grace* is about the application of the blood of Jesus and the power of the Holy Spirit—it is about the power of God's Word. It radiates with the joy, peace, and freedom from the accuser's accusations. Through God's Word, filled with unfathomable grace and love, our wounded souls are healed.

Covered by *Grace* is an illustration of how God relentlessly tracks us down even in the midst of ongoing sin—rescuing, cleansing, and bringing to us His restoration. He comes to reconstruct. His building materials—our own destruction and devastation. He freely gives to us new hope, renewed faith, full new abundant life, and triumphant victory.

INTRODUCTION

THE PROBLEM WAS *I* didn't believe it. Anguish accompanied the exposure of my hidden comfort zone. The inability to candidly face myself from the darkest of times and openly admit the long-ago sin was as it was: detestable, repugnant, and abhorrent required desperate measures. Could I ever be cleansed enough to blot out the scars of self-judgement and the deep-seated disappointment in myself, let alone fulfill God's purposes? My soul had become deeply wounded! Destroyed was my testimony, my reputation, and my future toward anything related to the Lord. Did even God have enough *grace* for the likes of me?

Fear and anxiety from my perception of impending threats loomed out of proportion towards being transparent with friends, colleagues, and loved ones. If they only knew. That darkened portion of history would cause me to be shunned, avoided, and rejected. Shackled by public opinion, I became terrified of what people would think. I believed a ring of accusing and condemning gossip would be endless and I permanently stained. I had claimed this offensive thing as "my sin." It held a grip on me, crippling my spirit. It had a grip upon my memories as well. I considered myself a deeply soiled person. Being hindered by a wasteland of enormous shame, even after repenting about forty years ago and receiving forgiveness from those I injured, five years have lapsed since the Lord requested I start writing about the one thing I knew quite well—His forgiveness.

Covered by Grace is a journal about a journey of seeking and receiving the fullness of God's forgiveness as well as the fullness of God's presence. It is about His healing *grace* and mercy through the many facets of God's provisions in the Old and New Testaments of the Bible. Even though we do not deserve it, it is about how God heals our inner being, our soul. It is about experiencing for ourselves the beauty within the length, depth, width, and height of God's incomprehensible love. It is about being covered by *grace* by an immense God of *grace* who loves you and me with an unfathomable measure of love. It's about God Almighty who will chase us down, climb the rockiest mountain, descend into the lowermost valley, and even meet us at our bed of death to simply redeem us with His *grace*. It's about God's truth. It's about moving beyond the stronghold of fear, especially the fear generated by the opinions of other individuals.

Inadvertently, from childhood, what was said with the best of intensions by loving adults who had my best interests at heart, became a paralyzing stronghold in my thinking pattern. *"What will people think?"* was enormously powerful as if their opinions meant life or death in addition to their opinions being better and far more legitimate than mine. However, it missed the mark toward being helpful with righteous decisions and inner confidence. Furthermore, it embedded copious amounts of fear into the equation. Being highly sensitive to what people would think or gossip about fostered a need to cover up what they might see in me as "bad." Of course, I wanted to be "good" but, I could never measure up or be as flawless as what numerous individuals had spoken over me. "You're so perfect, I bet you can walk on water!" was not usual for me to hear. Now, I was powerfully trapped in a different kind of sin. That sin being the foundation for *"stinkin thinkin,"* and compounding the intricacies of life.

God has been incredibly loving, kind, and patient as I gradually trusted and consigned to Him the keys for those doors locked with misguided beliefs. As He has revealed and mirrored the contents of my heart back to me over the course of time, I have risked the truth with more and more close friends, family members, and now you because the Lord has required me to share assisting others to find freedom from the darkness—from remorse and shame.

I loved the Lord, at least in thought. And, priding myself with knowing I was a good person with regular church attendance and available to help wherever needed was the making of a Christian. Being a bit legalistic, I held a long list of things I didn't do, like I didn't smoke or drink or cuss or swear; I worked for an honest wage. Yet, in a severely challenging time of life, the Ten Commandments were broken. When tested, I was not who I thought I was nor who I wanted to be. I was found to be wanting. I had failed the Lord. I had failed my family. I had failed my friends. I had failed in faith. I had failed in spirit. I had failed morally. I had failed myself. I had made decisions driven by hollow and deceptive human philosophies, elemental spiritual forces of this world rather than directed by Christ. Thus, the name of Jesus Christ had been given a "black eye" and essentially, I had rubbed His name in the dirt. I discovered I knew only facts and was powerless to live life as holy. I contained only a shallow appearance of Godliness.

Even though *Covered by Grace* continues as an unending journey of discovery, learning the length, height, width, and depth of God's love, the setting originates during my senior year of college after marrying my first husband.

We will discover throughout this journey how to continue living in favor with our Lord God Almighty. Also, we will learn how to run from the darkness of shame and remorse into the *glory light* of Jesus Christ. Finally, Covered by *Grace* is a living demonstration of how to receive and unremittingly live in God's astounding gift of forgiveness—His *grace*.

GRACE DEFINED

GRACE

"Grace and peace be yours in abundance through the knowledge of God and of Jesus our Lord" (2 Peter 1:2 NIV).

GRACE! GOD'S *GRACE* BURSTS forth unhindered with over-abundance through the fountain of His love. As the Lord embraces us with His *grace*, we in turn are enabled to reach out, not only to receive His gifts but also with expectant hands to touch His heart in return. Scripture confirms that *grace* has been given to each one of us according to the measure of Christ's gift (Ephesians 4:7). Even in the beginning when the earth was saturated in violence, evil, and corruption, Genius 6:8 tells us Noah had found *grace* in the eyes of the Lord. Thus, he and his family were saved. Furthermore, *grace* beautiful *grace* is voiced in Ephesians 2:7 "…in order of the coming ages he might show the incomparable riches of his *grace,* expressed in his kindness to us in Christ Jesus." The Lord told the Apostle Paul in 2 Corinthians 12:9, that His *grace* was sufficient for him. Not only sufficient—but His power is made perfect in our weaknesses. God's *grace* is surely sufficient for us as well.

Where sin abounds, *Grace* abounds even more!

Hence, what is *Grace*? Biblically defined, it is the unmerited, unearned, and undeserved favor and/or blessings from God, an inexpressible gift freely given! It is the influence or spirit of God operating within us to regenerate us. It is a virtue of divine origin. It is being in God's favor. All that we are promised in His Word comes to

us through His love. His essence is synonymous with His *grace*. No one of us deserves *grace* for all have sinned (Romans 3:23). We cannot earn *grace*, nor can we purchase it. Neither can we create it for ourselves.

We receive *grace* in the same manner that we receive salvation— by faith, taking God at His word and by the witness or testimony of the Holy Spirit within our spirit (Romans 8:16). It is the Holy Spirit who confirms when we have become children of God. You see, God sent His son as a marvelous gift into the world so that whomever believes upon Him shall live forever. He came not to condemn the world but that we might be saved, set free from the bondage of sin through Jesus Christ (John 3:16-17). Furthermore, the incomprehensible riches of his *grace* are expressed in his kindness to us in Christ Jesus (Ephesians 2:7).

God's *grace*, therefore, provides salvation (Romans 2:4). God's *grace* brings forgiveness (1 John 1:9). God's *grace* conquered our sin (Romans 5:20). God's *grace* reconciles us to Him while we were yet His enemies (Romans 5:10). God's *grace* exchanges deserved death for life. God's *grace* provides a new relationship of intimacy and favor with Christ (Exodus 33:17). God's *grace* lavishes upon us wisdom and insight through Christ (Ephesians 1:8 AMP). God's *grace* draws us near to His Throne with confidence to find mercy and help when we are in need of deliverance (Psalms 44:3-8; Hebrews 4:16). God's *grace* equips us to renounce ungodliness and worldly passions (Titus 2:11-14). God's *grace* comes searching for us (Luke 15:1-7). God's *grace* supplies us with immeasurable riches in kindnesses and unity with the brethren (Ephesians 2:7). God's *grace* causes us to acknowledge that we are His workmanship (Ephesians 2:10). God's *grace* lends to us faith (Romans 12:6). God's *grace* continually and actively works within us giving strength to do all things through Him (2 Timothy 2:1). God's *grace* enfolds us in comfort through His encouragement (2 Thessalonians 2:16-17). God's *grace* bubbles over within us with a spirit of thanksgiving (Ephesians 5:20). God's *grace* brings peace and contentment (Philippians 4:12). God's *grace* showers us with edification and encouragement (Philippians 4:13). God's *grace* draws us to abide continuously in Him (John 15:5 KJV). God's *grace* through the Holy Spirit draws us into the Word of God (John 12:32 ESV). God's *grace* causes us to hunger and thirst for righteousness (Matthew 5:6). God's *grace* inundates us with abundant life (John

10:10 ESV). The Lord desires that we live vibrantly. He desires we live radiant lives in our reflection of Him. God's *grace* ignites us with joy. His *grace* perfects us with the gift of the Holy Spirit giving us power and boldness in His service (Luke 11:13)! God's *grace* produces a giving and generous heart (Acts 4:32-34). God's *grace* bestows His peace upon us guarding our hearts and mind (Philippians 4:7; Psalm 29:11). God's *grace* heals our pain and prospers our soul (3 John 1:2). God's *grace* leads us into repentance and restores our soul (Psalm 32:1-5; Romans 2:4). God's *grace* radiates hope from deep within our soul (2 Thessalonians 2:16). And, out of His abundant *grace* flows immense mercy. Jesus has borne our judgement, allowing us to live uncondemned (Hebrews 4:16). God's *grace* is the Waymaker, blessings of *grace* upon *grace* (John 1:16 ESV).

With God's *grace*, the Holy Spirit—alive throughout the scriptures—infuses His Word (John 14:26) into our spirit providing healing to all our needs physically, mentally, emotionally, and spiritually. God's *grace* grants in us His wisdom (1 Corinthians 1:30). God's *grace* causes us to abound and excel (Hebrews 12:1-2) in His immense love compelling us to keep pace with Him as we run the race placed before us—regardless of our past failures as well as any failures in the future. It is with tremendous gratitude that we are covered by this all-inclusive *grace*.

In other words, *grace* encompasses all of what the Lord our God has for us. As Graham Cooke, mentor and author of *The Mentoring Track, Your Starting Point for Grace*, puts it, "*Grace* is the empowering presence of the Lord that enables us to become the person He has called us to be. Sheltering us from shame and condemnation, *grace* is what God sees in us as He looks at us in and through Jesus Christ." We will thrive in the freedom of God's ever living, perfect gift of love— His *grace*.

GRACE ILLUSTRATED

STAINED

Fear stormed from the depths of unbridled shame and rose up
like a torrent of killer bees on the attack.

Fear had her in its tight-fisted clutches, paralyzed. She could not
bear to see the truth for herself let alone expose it to the light.

It was as though her body had been bisected, to be emptied of
all its putridness, then carried like a callusing rucksack.

Would or could the stain buried deeply within
the pit of her soul ever be removed?
Doubtful… was the thought. She, after all, had been carrying this
rending burden for decades of time.

Transformed by the entanglement of guilt.

Exposure could damage her image. People would talk; they would
gossip, stare, point fingers, alienate her, press
her with their abhorrent labels,
hold her in disdain and capture her in condemnation.

Did God actually expect a public confession from her? Was God
wanting her story highlighted on the front
cover of all the popular tabloids?
What was the value?

Mary Berry

Surely it wasn't so! But, indeed, it did appear
as such, even though the sin
had been forgiven decades ago and buried in the deepest sea.

by MaB

TROUBLE BY THE TRUCKLOAD

We CHRISTIANS CAN GET ourselves into a truckload of trouble by unquestioningly trusting self as well as friends excessively. We lean toward forgetfulness. We forget to cover ourselves with the armor of God. We forget about righteousness during the parlay of merriment. We often assume that we are safely protected from enticement when we are in the company of trusted Christian individuals—all living within the Godly standards Christ has set before us. Deception blinds us into believing there will be no temptation among our trusted friends. Entrapment follows. From the condition of our heart, our mouths speak, and actions follow.

How can it be that knowing right from wrong is not enough to faithfully do the right thing? The Ten Commandments are straight forward and clear, both in the physical and in the spiritual realm. I mean, what can be misunderstood in "Thou shall not..."?

For those of us who raise children, I can imagine that we all have said something similar. Something like, "What do you not understand about the word, "No?" is common when rerouting a child's behavior.

In Deuteronomy 5:2 (HCSB), Moses relays God's decree to the people, *"Israel, listen to the statues and ordinances I am proclaiming as you hear them today. Learn and follow them carefully."*

Do not have other gods besides Me…;
Do not make an idol for yourself…;
Do not misuse the name of the Lord your God…;
Be careful to remember the Sabbath day, to keep it holy…;
Honor your father and your mother…;
Do not murder…;
Do not commit adultery…;
Do not steal…;
Do not give dishonest testimony against your neighbor…;
Do not covet…" (Deuteronomy 5:7–21).

It should be easy to follow ten simple straight forward directions. But, as it turns out, it is impossible when left to our own devices to be faithful. Human nature hasn't changed since those ten commandments were issued. Thankfully, God still directs our lives today. He asks each of us to walk the path He has prepared for us. I remember one individual stated, "If God asked me to do something, I'd jump right on it!" I had always thought so, too, until God required the impossible!

Initially, when the conception of this endeavor, writing Covered by *Grace,* transpired, I thrust my hands deep into the chasms of my jeans pockets while adamantly exclaiming to the Lord, "NO! I don't think so! I'm not exposing my shamefulness to the world!" Fear became overwhelming creating the heaviness of depression. Suddenly, abhorrent sins from the past loomed like bright neon billboards within my memory. Even though those sins had long ago been forgiven and buried in the deepest ocean and hidden as far as the east is from the west, they seemed to remain like thoroughly rotten, filthy, and sodden rags. They should never see the light of day much less be mentioned (Ephesians 5:12)! Despite the fact I had not purposed to do evil, nonetheless, evil prevailed.

Regardless, the Lord has asked me to share from that long-ago portion of my life to illustrate how His love does indeed freely cover a multitude of sins. Nothing remains hidden. In addition, through His great kindness, He desires for His children to forget the former things and attend to the needs at hand today, to move boldly forward in Christ, sharing the Good News. It is with sincere humility, humbleness and in obedience to the Lord, I share the goodness of His vast and endless love.

Since, according to Romans 3:23, *"we all have sinned and fall short of the glory of God,"* we are at liberty to address this topic as equals. Your sins probably look different than mine, but possibly you may feel the same way about them as I do about the sins of my past, even though they are forgiven. You may have had sins (forgiven or unforgiven) locked up in the closet of your heart for years in the attempt to keep them safe from public discovery as I have. You might be imbued with untold shame such as I am when placed in a position of disclosure. The risk of transparency is immense, it seems.

Let me insert this caution before we continue to speak of sin; we must be cautious to what we claim as ours. It is of great consequence when we refer to the sins we have committed as, "my sin." When we do this, that sin of yesterday begins to own us by forming a stronghold around us and locking our mentality onto the sin itself. We only need to own up and give the sin to the Lord, Jesus Christ. Through God's forgiveness, they are no longer our sins. It doesn't matter what the sin was or is, God's love covers them with His *grace* by the multitude! He takes them, covers them with the shed blood of Jesus Christ, and buries them in the deepest sea. The penalty is gone; He remembers them no more (Psalm 103:12-14)! He wants to transform our lives to live in the beauty of freedom from sinfulness. Hallelujah! He sees us through His blood, and He imputes His righteousness upon us as His beloved children. Our lives become filled with an abundance of joy when we surrender; when we say, "Yes, Lord, I surrender to your plans and directions for my life. As we call out every sin, ask for forgiveness."

As mentioned above, it doesn't matter what the sin was or is. However, it does matter what *we do* with the memory of these sins. First, it is imperative that we bring them before the Lord with an attitude of a repentant heart asking the Lord to forgive us of whatever the specific sin is. Second, it is extremely important to repent before those whom we have wronged. This action promotes the release of mental and spiritual congestion as well as the guilt lodged in our heart. In addition, it can initiate healing for the innocent ones as well. We pray, they will have the strength through the Holy Spirit to forgive us for the wrong we've done them. Thirdly, it is crucial for the woundedness in our soul that was created by our sin to be healed as well. More about this topic is found in one of the later chapters, Our Wounded Soul.

JUST ONE TINY BITE

$\mathcal{S}$IN. IT ALL BEGAN with the very first humans God created on this earth, Adam and Eve. Have you ever wondered what our lives would be like if Eve and Adam had not touched or not eaten from that forbidden fruit tree, the tree of the knowledge of good and evil, there in the center of the Garden of Eden? Or, what would have happened if Adam had simply but gently rebuked his bride by telling her, "No, God has told us not to eat of this tree's fruit." Or, "Stop admiring its beauty! Let's move away from this tree." Or, "Now, Eve, confess your disobedience to our loving Father!" Wouldn't it be wonderful to know what would have happened if Adam had taken the lead with words encouraging humble repentance? There are so many unknowns in this Genesis chapter three scenario.

Think about this. These two individuals visited daily with the Lord as He walked through the garden in the morning coolness. Surely, they had an endearing relationship. Didn't they understand that God, their Father, meant what He said when He gave Adam specific instructions not to eat of the tree of the knowledge of good and evil in the center of the garden? Confidently, Eve had even told the serpent that they were not supposed to eat of the fruit from this tree of the knowledge of good and evil and then added to God's word, that they were not to even touch the fruit.

Touching the forbidden moves temptation up a notch. It becomes increasingly effortless to trespass, right? Why was it so seemingly easy for them to disobey the Lord? Didn't they have everything anyone

could have wanted. Was it not like the greatest vacation ever? They were surrounded with immense beauty. They were even trusted to care for everything within the garden. Adam named all the animals as God brought them before him. They walked and talked with God Himself—in person no less, face to face! So, what happened here? Did they not know where they were, in the Garden of Eden? Could it be they had never gone to the garden gate and seen the barrenness of the distant land? Was the serpent like a novelty to them? Had they become so accustom to living the good life or so naive that they just trusted all the created beings to be friendly, honest, and thoughtful? Obviously, there was one thing they had never known—temptation. Could it be that therein lies the problem? What do we know with certainty about our strength in the Lord without our ideals being fully tested?

What we do know with confidence is that sin did indeed enter the garden that day—that day when the serpent deceived Eve, when she decided he was right, and God was wrong. She could see for herself that the forbidden fruit was indeed beautiful, and it did appear scrumptiously delicious. Not only did the fruit look inviting and good for eating, but she also believed Satan, the serpent who told her the opposite of what God had told them. He told her that she surely would not die. She would become like God knowing good from evil. Did she have a secret desire to be like God? Or, maybe Eve didn't fully understand why God had put a limit on her choices, thus fell into the trap that so often causes us trouble today—human rational! Can we even be remotely tempted to disobey if our heart is not involved and open to the enticement? Oh, why did she put her trust in that serpent? And, then, of course, she just had to share her discovery with her handsome husband. We know Adam was not deceived because the Word tells us God had forbidden the consumption of this fruit before Eve had even been created. But Adam, evidently smitten by his bride, chose that one tiny bite. How was Adam to know the burdens of life about to be placed upon them due to one wrong decision? Was he tempted beyond his power to say "no" to her loveliness? Disobedient, they both fell head long right into the most immense quandary ever generated (Genesis 2:4-3:24).

The spirit of rebellion does not have to be in full rage, truly, just one tiny subtle increment can derail the heart and set it on a tumultuous trek!

They were tossed out of the garden, their beautiful home, into a life of thorns and briars. Their disobedience changed everything for them. And, it changed everything for mankind ever since—including us.

However, even from this early date in history, from the very beginning, God in His vast depth of love and mercy, covered Adam and Eve with His *grace*. The Lord used animal skins to cover their nakedness, far better than the flimsy self-made fig leaves. Blood, an atonement for their sin, had been shed. A sacrifice had been made. God had forgiven their sin. Even so, the consequences were grave.

In fact, we humans are still reeling from that mistake all these centuries later. Furthermore, we continue to allow ourselves to be thoroughly injured and maimed by this same crafty, callous, and scheming serpent. Why have we not wised up to his deceptive manners and his aspiration to annihilate us, God's children?

Don't you think it is high time, way past time, to put this devious serpent in his place? Absolutely! He has created more than enough damage! He grinds salt into our wounds as he sits back, glorying in his pillage of us!

God, however, did not make us to be His puppets. He has given us a free will. It is up to us to be mindful, attentive and willing to pursue His precepts, His directions, and His Word. The Lord never manipulates, nor does He impose His will upon His children. He bids us to come. It's up to us to follow in surrender to the One who created us and loves us most, Jesus Christ!

What, then, do we do to defeat the enemy? There may be a number of actions we can take, but I'll mention just four things that through Christ we can accomplish. Of utmost importance, the first thing to do is to continually abide in Christ and He will abide in us (John 15:1-17). Second, we are commanded to stay alert! We are asked to pray in the Spirit on all occasions with all kinds of prayers and requests (Ephesians 6:18-19). Third, God desires that each of us be fully attentive to the substance of His Word. As we are directed in 2 Timothy 2:15, we are to study the Word to show ourselves

approved unto God. In addition, Hosea 4:6 blatantly states that God's children die (spiritually) when rejecting and being indifferent to His instructions. Bear in mind, God's Word is spiritual and can only be rightly discerned through the Holy Spirit. Much error is realized when God's Word is attempted to be defined by the carnal mind and through the philosophies of mankind (Colossians 1:9-14; 2:8). Fourth, remember our earlier thoughts about Adam, Eve, and their consequences. Even though they were unaware of God's armor as described in the New Testament, it is crucial for us to daily wear the full armor of God as instructed in Ephesians 6:10-17. We must be prepared and equipped to take our stand against our adversary's schemes. For our struggle is not against flesh and blood, but against the rulers, against the authorities, against the powers of this dark world, and against the spiritual forces of evil in the heavenly realms.

Thus, we can diligently begin placing the armor of God upon our soul and spiritual self. Start with the *belt of truth*. To defeat the enemy, we must know the truth of God's Word. Satan fills our mind with lies said deceptively with tactics twisting the truth. Therefore, it is critical that we know and continually strive to understand God's Word for it is the truth.

Following the belt of truth is *God's breastplate of righteousness*. We anchor it tightly across our chest covering our heart—the seat of our emotions, self-worth, and trust. The Amplified Bible defines righteousness as integrity, moral rectitude, and right standing with God. Furthermore, it is God, himself, who imputes His righteousness upon us by our faith in Christ (Philippians 3:9).

Next, we place *the shoes of the gospel of peace* upon our feet like a pair of army boots laced up, fitted snuggly and securely, giving us firm-footed stability in promptness and readiness to face the enemy as produced by the Gospel of peace (Ephesians 6:15; Isaiah 52:7 AMP). God gives us the motivation to continue our journey of sharing the good news of Jesus Christ despite the haranguing trill from the enemy saying its worthless, hopeless, impossible, and unnecessary.

The fourth piece of armor is the *shield of faith*. Satan's attacks repeatedly come in the form of insults, setbacks, and temptations; but this shield, our faith and trust in God, protects us from those flaming arrows of contempt.

The *helmet of salvation* is the fifth piece of armor and is vital to our success in battle. We must cover our head, our mind, to have right and proper thinking because the devil loves to cause doubt. He plots against us wanting us to believe that the Word is fickle, untrustworthy. He wants us to believe that Jesus Christ was just a man, a fake. He wants us to doubt our salvation, to doubt God's love, to doubt God's mercy and *grace*, as well as His goodness! Satan wants us to believe that *self* in all its brilliance has the suitable, viable solutions to life's quandaries and that we don't need God. The enemy tries to convince us that God's Word is fractured, inconsistent, contradictory, and little suited for today's world. He tries to deceive us by sublimely saying, "It's all fantasy; only the weak need a crutch like the Bible. Thankfully, the mind of Christ within us refutes all the lies.

Sixth, we take up the *sword of the spirit which is the word of God*. It is the only offensive weapon necessary. The Word puts Satan to flight! Remember when Jesus was being tempted by Satan at the beginning of His ministry? Jesus spoke the Word to negate him. It's recorded in Matthew 4:4, "*It is written…man shall not live by bread alone but by every word that comes from the mouth of God.*"

The power of God's Word is immense! Hebrews 4:12 states just how intense the potency of His Word is: "For the word of God is alive and active! It is sharper than any double-edged sword, it penetrates even to dividing soul and spirit, joints and marrow, it judges the thoughts and attitudes of the heart. Nothing in all creation is hidden from God's sight! Everything is uncovered and laid bare before the eyes of him to whom we must give account" (Hebrews 4:13). Let us study and memorize the Word so that we are continuously equipped and prepared to do battle with power from God's truth. The battle may be fierce. Our armor may become scratched, dented, and mangled, but we will be victorious conquerors! And, God will restore our armor amid the victory to fight yet another day!

Finally, after we have spoken God's word of truth to the battle at hand, we stand our ground firmly planted in faith. We stand strong in prayer, fully dressed in God's armor.

REFLECTION

How long has it been?
When did you last reflect upon the sin within?
Have you met it face to face?
Do you have the strength, the conviction to
place it all before the Lord God of heaven and earth,
the King of Kings, the Lord of Lords?
We know that to say we have not sinned
simply is not true (1 John 1:8).
The Word tells us
every single one of us have sinned
and have come short of the glory of God (Romans 3:23).
What secrets do you keep?
What holds you in defeat?
It is time to replace the staleness of your spirit with the
refreshing fragrance of the Lord.

by MaB

Secrets

"...You will not be able to stand against your enemies until you remove what is set apart" (Joshua 7:10-13).

$\mathcal{J}$OSHUA 7:12 CLEARLY EXPLAINS why we have spiritual failures. Whether we say it's our disobedience or it's our sin, the results are the same. Our strength to serve the Lord diminishes, our lives are in shambles, and we stand powerless while facing the forces of our enemy, the adversary—Satan. Furthermore, sometimes the enemy is simply oneself.

Sin, of course, isolates us from the Lord. Our indifference to His Word is especially loathsome to Him. God does not wink at our sin! According to numerous pastors (including my own pastor at Trinity Lighthouse Church, Raymond England) there are a few basic foundational reasons why secret sin is abhorrent to our Lord.

First, God does indeed see into the depths of our hearts. He is omniscient, all-knowing. He knows our words before we speak them. Nothing is hidden from God. If we try to conceal our sin, we will not prosper (Proverbs 28:13). It's pointless to attempt to keep our sins secret from Him. I'm not, however, suggesting a person should announce their sin/s to every listening ear. But I do believe we must repent, confess our sin to the Lord, and ask forgiveness from each individual whom we may have injured physically, mentally, emotionally, or otherwise as stated in an earlier chapter.

Another reason sin isolates us from the Lord is that our sinful, secret thoughts originate from the same source as sinful deeds. For example, Jesus said that hatred for a brother carries the same penalty as murder (1 John 3:15) and that lust is the essence of adultery (Matthew 5:27-28). These sins are considered the same in consequence; one is the beginning and the other is the fulfillment of the same thought. Thus, it is imperative that we take every thought captive and make it obedient to the Lord (2 Corinthians 10:5).

Third, the sin we try to hide, acting as if we're innocent, especially sears our conscience and paves the way for other character-damaging sins. It's the hypocrisy, the leaven of the Pharisees (Luke 12:1) that compounds or multiplies the hidden sin, leaving us in dire straits creating deep wounds within our soul.

Furthermore, and fourth, tragically, we cannot fulfill the ministry God has planned for us, as the sin greatly weakens our spiritual strength to serve Him.

Our appearance of sinlessness only lasts until God brings us to the litmus test. To live holy lives, we must allow Jesus to bring to light daily that which is buried within causing us to be guilty. It will bring us life abundantly and excellence of soul (2 Peter 1:3). The Lord will not allow us to hide our active unforgiven sin under the rug or in a locked closet for any length of time. The Lord desires for us to be devoted to Him. He desires to rescue us in times of trouble. Listen to this—God Almighty wants to give us *honor*, to satisfy us with long life and show us His salvation. He does answer us when we call upon Him (Isaiah 65:24; Jeremiah 33:3)! Can we dare to believe the King of Kings and Lord of Lords, the creator of the universe truly desires to honor mankind—even with all our shortcomings? The very thought simply takes my breath away! Shouldn't that alone cause us to turn from our wicked ways? Thankfully, even though God hates sin—He loves us—His creation enough not to leave us in our sinful condition. He says, be holy as I am holy (1 Peter 1:16 ESV).

UNDER THE RUG

Is IT SAFE TO admit our lives may not be what others see from the outside? Perhaps we carry the appearance of a life fully put together in such a way that we become the envy of our neighbors? Maybe our personal life is full of doubts and possibly hidden sin? As an imperfect individual, Christian or otherwise, we may live in dread, fearful that an undisclosed sin will inadvertently become public knowledge.

Of course, we can ask two questions, "From whom is sin hidden, and against whom have I sinned?" David, in Psalm 139:1-12, assures us that God Almighty already knows every breath we take. He has numbered the hairs on our head. He knows our thoughts from afar off, and He knows our words before we even speak them. What is done in darkness will indeed come to the light. And, Psalm 51:3-4 reveals to us that we have sinned against God. So, if we think we're hiding anything, we are deceived! God, our omnipresent and omniscient father, knows and sees all.

This fact in the yesteryears of my life, terrified me, especially the part of that scripture that states, "what is done in darkness will indeed come to the light." As I have come to allow the Lord to have full reign over my will as in disclosing portions of my life through *Covered by Grace*, it proves Psalm 139:12 to be true. Though there are excruciatingly painful moments, the Lord also brings peace, joy, and strength that pass all understanding.

Recently, one of those painful moments began with, "You need to include more personal details," observed one of this book's reviewers.

Immediately I bemoaned, "Oh Lord, I don't see how I can possibly reveal any more than what I've already disclosed. Surely, generalities are enough."

The following morning, I was just conscious enough to realize I was wrestling and arguing with the Holy Spirit. "No, I can not abase myself even further! No, I will not!" I agonized.

"Yes, you can," replied the Holy Spirit kindly but firmly.

"NO, I CAN NOT!" I retorted!

Again, the Holy Spirit responded, this time more resolutely, "YES, you can!" And, then sternly, but with compassionate encouragement, the Holy Spirit brought His mission to a close with a firm, "You will!"

Unrelenting twisting and turning continued in my body and spirit; I was becoming like a wrung-out wash cloth as the scene persisted.

Finally, as I awoke physically limp and exhausted from the struggle, surrender came like a long distant runner crossing the finish line. Weary but wiser, like the runner, flopping down onto the cool ground to catch his or her breath, trembling, I said, "Okay Lord." And scarcely breathing, whispered, "I surrender *all*." "I will trust you." Following the Lord can be a bit like eating a favorite dessert such as a slice of Country Cherry Pie ala mode—hearty, delicious, and perfectly sweet, with an occasional cherry pit.

On the other hand, even though hiding is only temporary, concealing our sin from people who erroneously act as if they believe they have never sinned is another story altogether. Because of their arrogant judgements, we fear their pointed accusations would create a devastating catastrophe within our soul, not to mention bring ruin to our lives. Those of us who fear reprisal are uncomfortable with confessing to the world or even to one close friend about the darkness that has lurked within or perhaps continues to be on the prowl.

Some of us may feel our sin has been so inordinately abhorrent that we cannot begin to put a label on it. For various individuals the disgrace is felt so profoundly we cannot even open our eyes to look at the sin face to face. So, we've swept it under the rug with an attitude that asserts, "I'll think about that tomorrow, maybe." Sometimes, we've taken an intense "face plant." As we hit the dirt, it knocks the wind right out of us causing us to stay down for a very long time. We hope and pray God will overlook it and that it will stay unmentioned and under the rug forever, forgotten.

Furthermore, some of us may continue to falter having been captured and held prisoner by a stronghold's clutch of shame, guilt, and remorse. We may have even shed bitter tears while seeking the Lord's forgiveness. Absolutely, God does forgive us when we come to Him in a spirit of true repentance, where our contrite hearts turn to Him and away from evil. Even so, the enemy's stronghold may continue to hold us in bondage like a vice grip, not necessarily to sin, but holds us as if frozen and paralyzed in spirit. We may remain motionless, unable to enter the warmth and security of the presence of God. Consequently, we attempt to disguise our powerless position. In the same fashion, every word of God becomes filtered and possibly not received. His word becomes drenched through the camouflage of a fearful heart.

Again, what holds us in bondage? Perhaps it's our soul, wounded not only from the sin but also from the shame coupled with fear of exposure and humiliation that prevents a long-desired healing. As stated earlier, it may be the ridicule, the shrouded gossip, the whispers, and sideway glances, along with finger pointing, that fuel the dilemma—a complexity of haunted memories in buried silence. So, we guard our soulful needs—preserved, protected, and hidden. Complicating our situation even further with our prideful thinking, we may fear losing status in society or in our church in addition to family and friends. We may even be deeply deceived, believing our sin doesn't matter—all this preventing our admission of guilt.

The Apostle Paul has good advice for us. He, being a strongminded, no nonsense, resolutely focused, and confident leader, has staunchly stressed, "As for me, it matters very little how I might be evaluated by you or by any human authority. I don't even trust my own judgment on this point." Paul knew that he had a pure heart; God was his only judge. He went on to elaborate, "So don't make judgments about anyone ahead of time—before the Lord returns..." (1 Corinthians 4:3-5 NLT). In other words, even though he recognized that he had been the chief of sinners, after his miraculous conversion experience through God's grace and mercy, he had simply put the power of God first and foremost. He was a new person with a renewed mind. He didn't look back.

GUILTY AND UNDONE

$\mathscr{T}$HE QUESTION IS: How do we become like the Apostle Paul, put our past behind us, and move along onto the path God has created for us as individuals? How do we stop thinking about the emotion of shame and the feelings that overwhelm our soul? How do we let go of the past? Numerous people say, "Just do it!" Seems a lot easier said than done.

Because I abhor my sinfulness and consider it a horrendous abomination, my admission to guilt is extremely difficult. Self-preservation plays a huge role in my reluctance as well. How is it possible that the very thing I intensely detest caused me to become undone?

Covered by Grace is about allowing the Lord to heal the woundedness of a deeply wounded soul instead of focusing on dreadful sins of long-ago yesteryears. *Covered by Grace* is also about finding strength to continue running, with all our might, the race (special individualized purposes) God has established for each of us since before the foundation of the earth (Ephesians 1:4-5; 2:10). We must finish that which God our Father has purposed and prepared for us to accomplish! Yes, we tripped. We skinned our knees and elbows something fierce; and we broke our legs as we plummeted off our towering pedestal of, dare I say, self-righteousness.

Thankfully, our Lord is gracious and merciful and overflowing with love and compassion for everyone, including His wayward children (Psalm 145:9). Not only does He overshadow us, He lavishes His *grace* upon us as He gently moves us onward leaving the dusty dangers behind. He covers us with the blood of Jesus Christ. What the devil meant for evil, God can recover and use for good (Genesis 50:20). Perhaps this truth is difficult to grasp. If so, we learn from Isaiah 55:7-9 that God's ways and thoughts are not our thoughts or our ways. God's ways are much higher than ours.

Therefore, it is time to step up and believe what God says about us instead of agreeing with the devious condemnation Satan plants in our soul. We are the sons and daughters of the Most High King endowed with the same heavenly authority given to Christ. What the Lord has begun in us will continue even as He calls us home (Philippians 1:6). *Covered by Grace* is written to lend a hand as we walk through the anguish of healing.

The Lord has provided me with tremendous encouragement, coaxing and nudging before being capable of tromping through the muddy brambles of this arduous route. God the Father, the Lord Jesus Christ, and the Holy Spirit presented loving compassion all along this journey of *grace*—a journey of more than thirty-five years. I share in hopes of displaying a means for whomever to escape from darkness and shame. Living life in the abundance of Christ's presence and love is our goal.

It is through profound and painful remorse that I reveal these things. In the history of my life, there were about four years when I had fallen into deception. I had slipped into a time of being "the other woman," secretly living a life that deserved stoning according to the Word of God. This forbidden relationship brought me into the throes of motherhood as well.

How could these actions possibly be true? I mean, it was not at all within my nature to be promiscuous or even purposefully flirtatious for that matter. Believe me, if this deceptive and invisible spirit of debauchery could be inherent within the depths of my soul, it could reside in just about every soul. How could my soul contain such evil?

Full of lofty ideals, I married late in the spring of my junior year in college. Marriage was supposed to be a beautiful sacred institution satiated with love and communion. That was the dream. Even though one is told that every relationship has difficulties, you don't really believe it. Marriage would be like heaven, no problems, no tears, and

no hardships. It would be full of smiles, laughter, appreciation, respect, honor, and awesomeness. Not so!

I, being far from perfect, was extremely shy and bashful and struggled with letting my genuine feelings be known. Getting my point of view to resonate with my husband of that time was quite difficult. It's not that my words were not heard, they simply were not powerful enough, thus they were usually rejected. Frustration and aggravation followed. It wasn't long before our relationship was tainted with heartless hostilities and dirty deeds.

Keep in mind the immediate information is how life was from my point of view during our thirteen years of marriage. We were not a good match as we brought out the worst in each other. In the end, after going our separate ways, communication became less hostile.

My husband, of those days, most likely would not agree that he was a party to abuse; it is a strong word. But, when a wife becomes so frustrated and angry that she rips her clothing right off her body and then into shreds, there's a massive problem. When a wife is so frustrated and angry that the dinnerware ends up in broken shards, could it be a pent-up reaction to continual verbal abuse? When a wife is so full of regret and fervently prays that her spouse would die, something is terribly awry. When seemingly every spoken word is used against her, she feels battered and abused.

Physically, he had yet to harm me, thankfully. However, there would be an event—years into the future—that would finally sever our rocky dysfunctional marriage. Unrestrained sin just multiplies; it knows no bounds.

You might argue, since I stayed in the relationship for thirteen years, it surely was not all that terrible. To be sure, there were some good moments. Additionally, my belief system would not allow me to divorce—at least not in the beginning. I believed: "once married always married." Consequently, I continued to strive toward forgiveness and make my relationship into a heavenly marriage.

In addition, after enrolling in a practical psychology class from a nearby university, I was equipped to better manage stressful situations. It armed me with the realization that I alone could choose, it was a choice, my choice, whether to take offense or not. The sting of nasty words didn't in themselves have the authority to take up lodging within my heart unless I allowed them. Again, I had to separate myself from the ugliness and control my thoughts. This new knowledge gave power to withstand numerous tests as opportunities to practice this skill were frequent.

On one such occasion, after being pelted with offensive devaluing words, I remembered to remain silent, focus on counting to ten keeping my muscles relaxed, giving my heated emotions a moment to cool down. Even though his disrespect would leave me feeling less valued than gutter garbage, this time I was able to lock my eyes on him, stay positive, and keep calm. Little by little, I learned that my calmness prevented his anger from being transferred to me. He, on the other hand, had to find other ways to dispel it. Usually, he held onto his angry mood, highly frustrated. Eventually, it would defuse. Learning that no one can *make* us angry gives us a choice decided involuntarily or purposefully.

Before enrolling in the psychology class, I had inadvertently allowed my husband's anger to seep into my spirit, causing me to react with terse words. This displacement of anger, once inflicted in me, allowed him to walk away from his torrent of verbal offenses as if there had never even been an altercation! He was free from his frustrations and anger because I had reluctantly become a receptacle for deposits of rotten rubbish. The class didn't change my husband; I, on the other hand, found a small token of hope.

Years later after a job transfer out of state, the time came when we purchased a small share in a delightful little business. My husband, already gainfully employed, didn't actively participate in this adventure. Frequently, I worked side by side with kind, friendly, and protective guys. One small minute step at a time, through friendship, laughter, comradery, and reciprocal attraction to one of these coworkers, my defenses were relaxed, then, eventually altogether broken. Through this man's caring casual conversations, I innocently answered inquiring questions concerning my marriage's private status. Sharing my deepest fears, my regrets, my woundedness, disappointments, and disenchantments with an available listening shoulder served only as a catalyst for Satan to spring into action. Being incredibly naive, I didn't realize what deceptively thin ice I was standing on.

Since that time, I have learned that even if a male coworker or trustworthy brother becomes a friend and makes one feel protected, loved, and appreciated, one must remember men still want to make things right, even the score, prove they're the better man. They want to be the hero that saves the lady in distress even if their choices are sinful. Furthermore, I learned I had not been paying attention to my emotional status. I had no idea that my heart's condition was wide open, available and waiting for an opportunity to be appreciated and loved. My loyalty and allegiance to my husband were replaced by another man who demonstrated a tender caring nature.

A slight touch of the hand turned into a hand held at length. A short friendly hug developed into an endearing embrace. A carefully planned, secret rendezvous began. One sin begot another. I had never lied so much in my entire life as in this relationship just to cover my whereabouts—shopping trips, daily routines, and work-related business! The lies were believed as truth by those near to me because I had always been truthful. Even after my husband had inadvertently discovered a generic motel receipt and I, thoroughly questioned, instantaneous and feasible alibis burst into mind. I didn't realize there could be such deviousness in me. Truly a shameful sizzling soap opera was being lived, even if it had not been my intention. Even the tabloid readers would have blushed.

Let me ask, what do you do when you find yourself in the grip of powerful temptation, whether emotional or any other situation? Do you have the presence of mind to back away? Do you pray? Do you allow the Holy Spirit to guide and direct you? Or do you consciously and purposefully set strong boundaries before temptations arise? Do you have a prepared non-offensive defense? Or, do you follow the common worldly philosophies? Do you flirt with temptations, anything that is not of the Lord's character? Do you choose what seems acceptable to society? Do you choose behavior that appears to match what everyone else is doing? Do you excuse your actions for apparent validity?

Thankfully, God loved me even in sinfulness. Over time and two beautiful children later, He intervened by continually and tenderly guiding me back into His loving presence, forgiven and uncondemned. Yet, even after repentance and though I knew I was forgiven, I felt as if I had committed an unpardonable sin. In Biblical days, my life would have been horrifically terminated—via stoning. I hated this detestable and abhorrent sinfulness. Being too ashamed, I did not reveal the total truth to anyone—not my brother, not my sisters, not my parents, not my aunts, uncles, cousins, and especially not my friends, and certainly not any of my pastors or those in church leadership. These loved ones had always told me how perfect I was. Therefore, I swept it under the rug. I couldn't bear to see their faces fall in disbelief and be ashamed on my account. Every time they loved on me with their words of sweet affirmation or gave freely of their hugs, I would chastise myself with the thought, "If they only knew." If they only knew the rest of the story, they would never receive me with such lovingness. They would surely turn their back on me."

Once, however, I did ask a visiting evangelist what his thoughts were about divulging or confessing information that would potentially damage a person's reputation. His thought was, "No, let the information rest." So, I accepted his advice and let it rest—for a time. No one other than the few innocent individuals who were devastated by my actions did I speak with concerning my loathsome actions—to confess and to repent. And, then, only because of being driven by my guilty conscious. Asking them to forgive me was impossible; it seemed to mock the seriousness of the situation, too insincere, and too easy to say compared with the pain of betrayal they suffered. Even though by the *grace* of God they, too, forgave me, I continued to royally condemn myself for more than thirty-five years! How could this treasonous truth ever be wiped out of my soul?

New fears became overwhelming throughout the years. What if others learned of my disgrace? Surely, there would be those who would ostracize me from every gathering. Every woman would look at me through piercingly suspicious eyes. I would be branded with the scarlet letter. Carefully, I guarded what I believed to be a secret the best I could in the back corner of the deepest closet in a box of stone labeled, "Guilty!" Inadvertently, my soul was becoming more deeply wounded as it was held captive in the grip of the enemy's tight-fisted stronghold. Shame, regret, remorse, humiliation, and despair squeezed hard and attempted to drain me of all value. Perhaps you have felt similarly while in a position of sin and woundedness.

Never in a million years would I have publicly confessed these sins. Be that as it may, the Word of God teaches us that obedience is better than sacrifice (1 John 2:4-5; 1 Samuel 15:22-23). Simply because the Lord has asked me to write, even at the expense of deep abasement, I write. Admittingly, it has been a process of obedience! Demolition of dark locked closets through many interpreted dreams and prophetic words revealed the hidden parts of my soul to me. Pretty, not a trace! But deep within my soul, courage was gaining momentum—no longer a slave to fear.

Through it all, desiring the presence of the Lord Jesus Christ is treasure far more valuable than hiding in one's pride. For, in the presence of the Lord, there is joy untold and at thy right hand there are pleasures for evermore (Psalm 16:11)!

It's not so much the sin that the Lord asks me to discuss, but His immense depth of love illustrated in the great lengths He goes through to rescue us from the pit of destruction. *Covered by Grace* is written to display the depth of God's *grace.* It is written to demonstrate God's unfathomable forgiveness; and *Covered by Grace* is written to illustrate the height, width, depth, and length of God's love for all His children (Ephesians 3:18-19 AMP).

The parable about the one sheep that wandered away comes to mind. Jesus questioned the crowd, "What do you think? If a man has a hundred sheep and one of them wanders away, does he not leave the ninety-nine on the mountain and go in search for the one that is lost? And if it turns out he finds it, I assure you and most solemnly say to you, he rejoices over it more than over the ninety-nine that did not go astray. (Matthew 18:12-13 AMP). Oh, how He loves you and me!

The Lord loves His children to the point that, like a bloodhound, He tracks us down, leaving no rock unturned. He climbs the highest mountains, travels through the deepest valleys, and shines His Glory light into every darkened crevice. Then comes the jubilation! Jesus was quite serious when He stated He rejoices over us when He is received back into our hearts, and He safely returns us to the fold. As we actively abide in Christ, He mends our injuries, heals our hurts, and washes us white as snow. Are you among the "ones," the one that the Lord rejoices over?

SIN

Sin takes you places
you thought you would never go
and holds you captive
longer than you
ever thought possible!

Author unknown

PURSUED

*T*ODAY, I DELIGHT IN being loved enough by the Lord that He would step into my world of sin, rescuing me. Instant, it was not. No, it was more like displaying the artistic beauty of fly fishing where you enter the stream wearing your water waders, gracefully throwing out your length of line seamlessly arching and looping staying the course in midair with an attachment of a spot-on lure. The line lies with quiet precision across the water's surface; and you, anticipating the trout's attention, watch like an eagle for just the right moment of movement. Craftily and carefully, the line, with its prize, is orchestrated by the master through the river's current into a waiting net.

God had to get my full attention. And, it came in small increments. Sharing briefly God's power of rescue and deliverance from that defiling relationship and journey into the wilderness accentuates our Lord's immense love and amazing *grace.*

One of the first things on God's agenda was to take my husband and I out of the country for a year and a half. Perhaps we were supposed to grow closer, depend upon each other in new surroundings, new customs, new language, new people, and even share in the birth of a beautiful baby. For certain, it was a time of change. A time of growing. A time of learning. A time of refocus.

Yet, my heart was full of and spilling over with strong resistance. An adapted old adage, "You can take the girl out of the relationship, but you can't take the relationship out of the girl." just about explains everything. I did not want to be there in spite of the fact that my bucket list included travel and visiting other countries. Now, alone in this foreign country with someone I didn't trust was worrisome. But, even more worrisome was being isolated so far from home, so far from the relationship I had come to depend upon.

In addition, that feeling only enhanced the anxieties that naturally come along the path of a first pregnancy. Who does one talk to for guidance? Obstetrics wasn't quite the same as at home, was it? There were many "what if..." questions left unanswered. And, others answered by reading the few available baby books—the source of information in those days. Even while being uncooperative and unwavering, God, it seemed, was handing out blessings to me in particular. In time, and with the comradery of the English speaking Baptist missionaries and special liaisons, we were blessed with amazingly wonderful medical care, a superb specialist, and new friendships to whom I still feel indebted.

Slowly, my heart began to see the importance of choosing to live within God's plan and seek His direction. At least it was a beginning, albeit a meager one. The Lord and I began a new relationship. In time, He would become my protector, my peace, my inner joy, and my defender.

Soon, I was to learn just how much the Lord loved me and how the work of the supernatural can depend upon the cooperation from the physical. God's *grace* is ever so much more than what any of us deserve.

A soft voice in my inner being said, "Pray around the yard." My response was, "I will not pray with my husband, period." Of course, we were not getting along; praying with him seemed too much like surrender. On two other occasions the Lord's quiet voice requested that I pray around the yard. Finally, I submitted and replied, "Okay, as soon as my husband gets home, we will pray around the yard."

He had yet to return that darkened evening when an abrupt blast of broken glass sharply pierced the quiet. After regaining my shaken senses, it was alarmingly clear the sound was coming from the side entrance door. The door at the top of the patio stairway that opened into the small sitting room that separated me from my four month old sleeping baby. In a panic, my mind raced wildly. "What to do? Can't call the police. Can't speak the language. Can't run to a distant neighbor, too far and cannot leave my baby. Can't run out the front

door, an accomplice or wild dog could be readying for me." Finally, I remembered a group of people had prayed over us before leaving the states and undoubtedly were faithfully continuing their prayers. Philippians 2:10 seemed paramount, "that at the name of Jesus every knee should bow, in heaven and on earth and under the earth." After mentally rehearsing the verse numerous times—silence. Relieved and thankful at how quickly and easily the quiet returned, I stood behind an inner doorway, hidden, but just a few feet away from where the shattering noise had come.

Now, for some reason, both hands raised above my head as if reaching for the sky as I rounded through the doorway and walked right up to and directly in front of the would-be intruder. He had one knee up, ready to crawl through the gaping empty door panel absent of its glass. As this scene registered, adrenaline, like a volley of electricity, coursed through my being, thoroughly paralyzing the senses. Hysterically, I tried shouting repeatedly, "In the name of Jesus Christ, get out!" "In the name of Jesus Christ, get out!" "In the name of Jesus Christ, get out!" The words were not discernable in English nor any other language for that matter. They were garbled nonsense to my ears. Finally, looking down, my gaze fell upon the largest saucer-sized dark brown eyes I had ever seen. Those eyes were locked onto something above me and held in complete astonishment and fear, and he still frozen in motion. All the while, my arms remained up and out and above my head. The man gradually came-to and slowly lowered his leg, slowly stepped backwards, down each step, not taking his eyes off whatever it was that kept his rapt attention and me not taking my eyes off him. However, once he hit the landing on the patio, he shot off like a terrorized maniac.

As a side note, I'm quite confident that man has a story to tell. I often wonder if he ever told anyone about his interrupted intrusion. Obviously, it was a terrifying experience for him as well as for me. Having seen a heavenly being, my guardian angel, would definitely be an extreme experience for anyone living in this physical world. Surely, the angel had overshadowed me. Me, so undeserving, yet immensely grateful.

The realization that the Lord had not asked my husband to pray came many years later. The direction to pray was given to me alone.

In my weakness, I just thought he, being the head of the household, was required to pray this type of prayer just as we had prayed inside the house. If I'd only been more timely in obedience, this crisis would never have happened. Working out the aftermath of fear factors would not have been necessary either. However, I wouldn't have known the power within God's word.

It's not that we loved God, but that He first loved us (1 John 4:19). Even in our greatest failures, the Lord continues to demonstrate His love because that is who He is. He is a good good Father reaching out to bring us close. His ways are not our ways (Isaiah 55:8-9). God's warmth and love would fully transform and win my heart once again.

With great appreciation, I am ever so thankful God in His mercy and love and *grace* came to my rescue. Oh, what a good good Father He is! He holds me, us, under the pinion of His wing when we ask (Psalm 91). He places chariots of fire in the atmosphere overhead heralded by the very hosts of heaven to protect His beloved.

After returning to the states, God's love simply continued to pursue me in every breathing moment. The Holy Spirit began and continued over time to gently nag me by filling my conscience with thoughts of, "You're making serious mistakes." "This association is not for you." "Come away from this." "This is not the way." and "This is wrong."

Eventually little irritations would arise in the relationship causing me to feel annoyed or disappointed, and then in due course wanting more than anything to bring the bond to an end. As time went on, I was going home emotionally empty and alone. The relationship fell short—it was incognito. A relationship disguised just cannot bring lasting satisfaction or joy. Covering one's tracks, making excuses, always looking over your shoulder grows weary. Ultimately, it fell short of every possible expectation. Essentially, it was a one-way street headed toward a dead-end. More sorrow, layer upon layer, was growing. Toward the end of the relationship, I began to put out a fleece before the Lord. Of course, and without apology, the Holy Spirit created events to go in His favor! I was edging closer and closer to God's handheld fishing net about to be fully rescued. Furthermore, several short ministry moments would catch my attention as I listened to a local Christian radio station's symposium.

One of those programs enlightened what was taking place within my soul. I saw myself for the first time as a statistic which caused me to see the sinfulness in a whole new dimension. Psychologically speaking, my heart and spiritual condition had been ripe for the picking. And, I had spiraled right into a predictable and treacherous pit. In other words, I had been a sitting duck. Whatever the deception, it was now exposed. And, I hated what I saw. Clearly, there was fallacy in thinking that this relationship had any potential of growth or lasting love. God brought me to attention! My attachment in this relationship was unhealthy spiritually. It was unhealthy physically. It was unhealthy emotionally. And, it was unhealthy relationally, not to mention being completely unrighteous for both parties.

The grass was not greener on the other side of the fence, meaning there are personal issues and challenges that must be dealt with on both sides of a relationship. There will always be two points of view—his and mine like two sides of a coin. That's a given. Perhaps we merely choose to ignore the work required to maintain that look of a perfectly cultivated lush lawn on our neighbor's side of the fence. Perhaps we only see the surface, the exterior of that other individual making it appear as if a relationship with them would make life a utopia. We may be coaxed into believing that the perfect relationship would automatically come about if we just had that other person as our spouse, and it does seem so by simple comparison. But do we know all the indiscernible facts, the ones that lie behind closed doors? Two factors imperative for spectacular relationships involve *mutual respect* and *honor* for each other, especially during the onslaughts of conflicts and struggles. One's partner should never be viewed as the "garbage bag" in any manner. Believing the rationale that married life would be splendid, free of issues, is like believing in fairy tales where everyone simply lives happily ever after. I had believed in fairy tales.

Even though what I had been reaching toward felt like comfort and solace and even though it felt wonderful to be treated kindly and tenderly like with the soft smoothness of satin and the richness of velvet, it was still sin. One could not change that fact! For a time, our connection was based on the needs perhaps of two empty hearts, hearts that could only be filled and satisfied through the love of Jesus, not each other. It was time for change. It was time to bring the sinful relationship to an end. It could never be lived joyously as it was woefully wrong. Sadly, it was also a horrendous statistic! What the enemy had come to do through my hapless choices, he did well. He had come to *steal, kill, and destroy* (John 10:10).

Perhaps your sin looks different. But, do you continue to find yourself in a similar snare choregraphed by the enemy?

It is made crystal clear in 1 Corinthians 6:9 (AMP) that we are not to be deceived. The unrighteous ones will not inherit the Kingdom of God. And then a rather long list of what is considered by God to be unrighteous is listed. The verse continues, "Do you not know that your body is a temple of the Holy Spirit who is within you, whom you have [received as a gift] from God, and that you are not your own [property]? You were bought with a price [you were actually purchased with the precious blood of Jesus and made His own]. So then, honor and glorify God with your body."

The resounding advice from the ministry moments was twofold but quite simple: One, admit your guilt to a trusted counselor, pastor, or friend as well as your spouse. (But this was not a sound option in my case. Promises to keep this relationship confidential were paramount.) However, once confessed, the enemy's stronghold could be broken. The other was to "move away, stay away, and never allow yourself to be near this individual again." In other words, "run for your life!" Because, indeed your life is at stake!

Several months later, I did this very thing. I left with my young children, leaving behind all entrapments, and returned to my parents' home, for a time while I furthered my education and reestablished my roots. My childhood home was rich in love, grace, and the peace of God—a perfect place to begin again now as a single mom of two.

It is important to not only move away but also remove tangible memories in order to break the unrighteous soul ties. What is a soul tie? A soul-tie is created through a personal and intimate relationship. A person has fully given themselves, spirit, soul, and body to another person forming a union, a bond, like glue. It will hold you to the other individual for a lifetime, whether you want it to or not. It's the spiritual nature, the affect, of intimacy. If the relationship is severed, portions of the bond continue to remain with each person. These ties, if unholy or unhealthy, as in the relationship of an affair, can even drive your

thinking and personality long after the relationship has been dissolved. So, you can see why it is imperative to destroy unhealthy, unholy, or unrighteous soul ties. Thankfully, there is nothing too difficult for the Lord (Jeremiah 32:27; Luke 18:27).

Decades later, long after re-establishing my life in the strength of the Lord, I was introduced to Evangelist Billy Burke from World Outreach Healing Ministry, Tampa, Florida. As a visiting evangelist for a few evenings, he led our congregation through the power of the Lord into awesome teaching and healings. On one of the evenings, he spoke about the topic of breaking soul ties. Emphatically, he declared that it is imperative to get rid of all gifts, especially clothing, jewelry and pictures given by a wrongful partner. These seemingly small things have an inordinate bonding power between the giver and the receiver, creating a spirit of union through our memories and spirit. In other words, "they serve to seal a contract of unrighteousness with the devil," warns Eddie and Alice Smith in *Spiritual Housecleaning: Protect Your Home and Family from Spiritual Pollution (2015)*. Again, regardless of the monetary value or beauty of these items, they must be removed, thrown away, or returned.

Even though I had long ago removed most all the tangible items (there had only been a few), I still had one in my possession, a blue ceramic music box. I had purchased it via a gift of cash. I had held onto it not necessarily because of lingering attachments from memories, but simply because it was beautiful—I liked it! Nevertheless, I could feel the nudging from the Holy Spirit to remove it. It had to go as well.

It doesn't matter whether an item is purchased by oneself through a cash gift or lovingly given by the partner. Nothing should be left in the physical world to separate us from the strength and power of the Lord. Likewise, nothing should be left in our spirit that would separate us from the strength and power of the Lord. Letting go of the root of our desire, removing it by the blood of Jesus and in the name of Jesus Christ, King of Kings and Lord of Lords, is just as important as letting go of items in the physical world. It is imperative! Wrongful soul ties operate to give the enemy an open door not only to bring condemnation upon us but also to cloud our minds with mire and impure remembrances of past actions as well as to create new impure offenses. Besides that, these wrongful soul ties weaken not only our worship but also the effectiveness of our prayers. Let me ask, "Who gains from this weakness, the Lord, or the enemy?"

Simply stated, we are like vessels. What we receive from study, from worldly interactions, from electronic connections such as television programs and web sites, from relationships, from failures, from friends, from teachers, from pastors, from parents, from the Lord, and from whatever source, there is a spiritual filament attached—some righteous and others not so much! All these filaments accumulate into and fill our vessel. We become a creation of all that has been deposited within us. If we are to be a vessel of honor for the Lord, the influence from the impure filaments must be removed (2 Timothy 2:21).

Yet, in those earlier days of when I had returned to my parents' home to begin again, not only on a personal level but also as a college graduate student commuting to the nearest university carrying an overload of required classes, I discovered breaking soul ties was a process. Being productively occupied with course work was one effective means to assist in keeping my mind focused, looking ahead, and giving maximum attention to necessary successes. It took much determination. Even so, real power was beyond self-control; it also took much prayer. It took trusting and acknowledging that God had a better plan even while often debating the need for leaving soul ties behind. Once the enemy has a hold on us, he will do everything he can to maintain his iron-claw grip. We must do battle to break free.

As expressed in Ephesians 6:10-20, the Lord directs us to be strong and mighty in His power. He says, "Put on the full armor of God, so that you can take your stand against the devil's schemes. For our struggle is not against flesh and blood, but against the rulers, against the authorities, against the powers of this dark world and against the spiritual forces of evil in the heavenly realms. Therefore, put on the full armor of God, so that when the day of evil comes, you may be able to stand your ground..."

Wearing the armor of God became a standard when dressing for the day and especially when preparing for sleep. Always stating aloud, I would repeat: "I place the helmet of salvation on my head for right and proper thinking with the mind of Christ, the breastplate of righteousness over my heart and chest, and the belt of God's truth around my waist. I place the shoes of the gospel of peace upon my

feet. I take the sword of God's word in my right hand and the shield of faith in my left ready to do battle." Then I would plead the "blood of Jesus" upon my conscious and subconscious mind. The results were astounding! As I gave God permission, he continued to chip away at my wrongful attachment until it was completely gone.

Another essential key was to avoid communication, physically and mentally, with the relationship. No daydreaming about the past is allowed. As thoughts would attempt to distract me, I would crowd them out by singing in my off-key voice of taking one day at a time except the duration of one day seemed too long of a stretch; so I would sing, "Moment by moment Lord, hold my heart and mind in your care."

Knowing I would be free from this entanglement of the enemy's design eventually brought a sense of resignation and peace. God was taking me gently and lovingly step by step up a higher road.

A fourth means of removing soul ties was through scripture. Jeremiah chapter one verse twelve explains that the Lord continually watches over His Word to perform it. One scripture that grabbed ahold of me was Ephesians 3:14-20. It became and continues to be incredibly powerful, causing deep spiritual growth and change.

Repeating this Word prayerfully aloud was monumental to changes within my spirit and soul. My favorite version is from the Amplified Bible. If you would like, join me now being careful to personalize. Change the personal pronouns "you/your/us" to "*I or me*," however it fits grammatically:

> *"For this reason [grasping the greatness of this plan by which Jews and Gentiles are joined together in Christ] I bow my knees [in reverence] before the Father [of our Lord Jesus Christ], from whom every family in heaven and on earth derives its name [God—the first and ultimate Father]. May He grant you/me out of the riches of His glory, to be strengthened and spiritually energized with power through His Spirit in your/my inner self, [indwelling your/my innermost being and personality], so that Christ may dwell in your/my heart through your/my faith. And may you/I, having been [deeply] rooted and [securely] grounded in love, be fully capable of comprehending with all the saints (God's people) the width and length and height and depth of*

His love [fully experiencing that amazing, endless love]; and [that you/I may come] to know [practically, through personal experience] the love of Christ which far surpasses [mere] knowledge [without experience], that you/I may be filled up [throughout your/my being] to all the fullness of God [so that you/I may have the richest experience of God's presence in your/my lives/life, completely filled and flooded with God Himself]. Now to Him who is able to [carry out His purpose and] do superabundantly more than all that we dare ask or think [infinitely beyond our greatest prayers, hopes, or dreams], according to His power that is at work within us/me, to Him be the glory in the church and in Christ Jesus throughout all generations forever and ever. Amen."

In addition, being related to scripture, beginning a personal Bible study, Woman of Excellence, A Bible Study by Cynthia Heald (1986), proved to be immensely powerful.

Developing into a true daughter of the Most High God had become paramount. Pouring God's word into my soul and spirit gave me layers of spiritual strength. The past sins were behind me. These increments of cleansing did more than remove soul ties, they developed into a lifestyle—choosing to live for the Lord willingly and joyfully, daily.

Grace is so amazing. The Lord has mysterious ways of cajoling us into obedience and submission, it seems. During my moments of protest, and while my fears paralyzed me, when I finally resigned and simply lifted my hands and my soul in submission, *grace* took over. God supernaturally gives us power, strength, and a willing heart. The Apostle Paul described this when he explained, "For God is the One working in you, both to will and to do His good pleasure" (Philippians 2:13).

So how do we continue to live in favor with our Lord God Almighty? How do we move from the darkness of shame and remorse into the Glory Light of Jesus Christ?

YOUR PRESENCE LORD

$\mathscr{S}$TAYING IN THE PRESENCE of the Lord is paramount to successfully and consistently living our lives in holiness. Daily covering ourselves with the armor of God prepares us for the evil day (Ephesians 6:13). Being ready to delve into spiritual warfare at the first hint that Satan is prowling nearby, and when is he not, will save us much anguish. Of course, a Christian would think of this as common sense, but it's not always applied.

Time passed. Upon finishing my graduate program, relocating to a new position of employment brought me to a new town as well as to dedicated involvement in one of the local churches. The words spoken by the pastor as he addressed the congregation with the Lord's message were as sweet as honey, easily enrapturing my spirit. Growing in the strength of the Lord was all that mattered. Here, in this town and church, where everyone was a stranger, new friendships were gradually established. One became a precious prayer partner. This Christian lady was indeed a warrior in whom I could trust to pray confidentially and whole heartedly concerning every issue and situation, including those that required steadfast spiritual warfare.

Now, the test was at hand. The relationship I left had come to pay a visit while traveling through the area on business. I had asked this prayer partner to keep me in the hand of God before meeting with this gentleman. Then I applied the armor of God to my spiritual being. I would be reminding him of Ephesians 5:5-6 even though he would not want to hear it.

Necessary endings are paramount for moving forward. Even though I deeply cared for this man, I was long past being part of the debauchery created by a wrongful relationship. He had to know the ending had indeed come. My desire was to be holy in every relationship. So standing firmly in God's strength, dressed in His armor, it was now possible to be in this person's company, yet not sin. No, it was not easy; we were not on the same page, sort of to speak. Holding his hands firmly in mine, looking eye to eye, he had to listen to God's words.

> *"For be sure of this, that no person practicing immorality or impurity in thought or in life... has any inheritance in the kingdom of Christ and of God. Let no one delude and deceive you with empty excuses and groundless arguments [for these sins], for through these things the wrath of God comes upon the sons of rebellion and disobedience" (Ephesians 5:5-6).*

He received God's Word as a gentleman. Hallelujah!

Later, the following morning, within a vision I saw myself laying bone tired, wholly exhausted, immersed in a ditch full of tall grass alongside the roadway. My armor was deeply dented, tarnished, and in frazzled disarray when, suddenly, it popped right back into fresh brilliance! I was alive and vibrantly victorious! Hallelujah! Being determined not to turn back, the battle for righteousness had been fierce.

Wearing God's daily armor proved powerful. Misunderstandings and misinterpretations happen. But let me point out, a friendly "Hello" to a man (single or married) from a lady, does not equate an invitation to cuddles, hugs, or snuggles. Most likely the honest smile is simply a means to sharing God's love. As we bring every thought captive to the will and purposes of God, the glory of the Lord is made manifest.

Sin destroys our relationships with each other and with the Lord. Thankfully, our Lord saw our need for redemption. God knew we owed a debt we could never pay; so He sent His beloved son, Jesus Christ, to pay that debt for us (John 3:16).

Since God is perfect in all His ways, it seems as though He would want only perfect, sinless individuals to serve Him, accomplishing His purposes. However, the Lord has shown us example after example

through people of the Bible, in both the old and the new testaments, how they served Him well despite their human weaknesses, shortcomings, and failures. We remember the Word states, "My power is made perfect in weaknesses" (2 Corinthians 12:9). God in all His wisdom sets the standard of perfection requiring only a broken spirit and contrite heart (Psalm 51:17). Since He has chosen you, then you are the one, perfect, to complete the task He has called you to accomplish. Thus, we continue in our walk with the Lord.

ISN'T KNOWING ENOUGH?

$\mathscr{B}$EING CALLED TO THE task is not the same as being sinless through the walk God has given us as we shall see with the following men. What is the difference between King David and King Saul? King David is the man who plotted murder and committed adultery. King Saul lost his sons as well as his kingdom for not listening, one too many times, to the words of the Lord (I Samuel 9-15; 2 Samuel 1-17). Both sinned. Yet God called David, "a man after my own heart." And, then there is Moses who murdered one of Pharaoh's soldiers but became one of God's most famous and faithful servants and he was considered "a friend of God" (Exodus 2:11-15; 3:1-15). Samson became disobedient and lost his eyesight and his mighty strength, yet God used him mightily toward the end of his life (Judges 13-21). Peter, one of Jesus's devoted disciples, denied ever knowing Jesus three times, then became one of the most powerful preachers of the Word in the early church (Luke 22:54-62). We should remember the Apostle Paul as well. Paul called himself the chief of sinners. As a Pharisee, he had been a terrorist and the murderer of countless believers of Jesus Christ (1 Timothy 1:15); but he became a dynamite man of God and wrote thirteen of the twenty-seven books of the New Testament!

Why did these great men of God sin? After all, these men were called and equipped by God. Was it because they did not know the law? Could they not discern between right and wrong? Can we excuse their sin by saying, "They're just human?" Could it be these six men were not so watchful; maybe they didn't pay attention to the voice of

God, or possibly they were not sober minded? Were they in collusion with worldly godless thinking? Or, perhaps we could chuck it off under the old cliché, "the devil made them do it." Perhaps it is true, in part anyway, because 1 Peter 5:8 commands us, "Be alert and of sober mind. Your enemy the devil prowls around like a roaring lion looking for someone to devour." Satan detests the children of God! He does everything he can to destroy us—whether it be physically, emotionally, with worldly thinking, with ill repute, or with condemnation. He will stop at nothing to annihilate us.

Still another thought: could it be that their attitude was similar to ours here in the twenty-first century regarding daily routine, rules, and laws? It has been said that our degree of attentiveness to our civil law has a direct reflection and correlation to our obedience to Jesus Christ, our Lord.

How many times in the distant past, for example, have we taken offense against various traffic laws? The posted interstate speed limit may be seventy miles per hour (in some states) but, we convincingly inform God, "I'm not actually speeding because seventy-five miles per hour is the allowable limit, and besides that, check out all those drivers who are passing us left and right!" Are we to pay attention to all directions, even a posted seemingly senseless speed limit of a snail paced fifteen miles per hour to round a simple bend in the road? Seriously! We ask, what does it matter? And, then we justify our actions accordingly! Does a stop sign and/or red light really mean stop, or just merely yield? How easy it is to thoughtlessly zip down the street with our thoughts drifting onto our lengthy to-do-list ignoring the warnings! Stop. Slow down. Caution. Construction Zone. Turn around, go back! After all, we have things to, do places to go, and we can't be late! Are we too preoccupied with our own desires? We seem to live with the motto, "Thanks anyway, God; but I've got this!" In like manner Proverbs 16:17-19 (HCSB) instructs us to remember, "pride comes before destruction, and an arrogant spirit before a fall." Instruction from Proverbs 3:5-7 tells us, "not to lean upon our own understanding; in all our ways submit to Him, and not to be wise in our own eyes. God will make our paths straight."

Could God's mighty men have had an arrogant spirit? Did they secretly think they had a better handle on the realities of life than God Almighty? Perhaps. Are we, today, any different?

In relating to this question, I remember believing it was impossible to restore or even bring the slightest change to my marriage. Furthermore, I wasn't going to give God an opportunity to even attempt to bring us into alignment. I had made up my mind. I wanted nothing more to do with the vastly difficult 13-year-old relationship. In fact, I was repulsed by the very thought of restoration. Divorce would finally dissolve the daily discord of incompatibility. We did attend a few counseling sessions at my parents' request, as they were deeply puzzled and questioned our motives. They had raised me to be of perfect moral standard; divorce was not an option. One dear friend tried to convince me to work out the problems. My brother and sisters didn't exactly understand but were supportive. Even though they all knew a great number of the reasons for turning to divorce, none of them were privy to the whole story; they had not walked in my shoes. They did not know every detail because I could not bear to expose my own faulty sinfulness. I could not bear to see their loving faces become jaw-drop, stoic. It was overwhelming enough that I could imagine in my mind's eye how they most likely would respond—in disbelief, disappointment, disgust, and possibly with angry condemnation. Furthermore, my pride would not allow me to position myself along with those "other" sinners and carry a disgusting label of debauchery or adultery.

In my younger years, I had heard and taken to heart the gossip concerning those who lived with lesser standards. Right along with everyone else, I had condemned those individuals. Now, it felt as if my own ridicule was boomeranging back towards me with deadly force. In addition, the overwhelming fear of public chastisement and criticism, perhaps even being ostracized by those who truly mattered in my life, was more than I could manage. One of those old family clichés, "You make your bed, and you lie in it," accused me and ranted repeatedly through my psyche. Numbers 32:23 summarizes things well by promising, "your sins will find you out!" I had never thought it remotely possible that this broken commandment would be a part of *my* life, so I did my best to hide it.

Why is it that knowing a specific action or deed to be sinful is not always enough to keep us from acting out in that sin? Even the Apostle Paul in Romans 7:15 mussed over his own actions, saying in effect that the very thing he doesn't want to do he does. I have no idea what his struggles were, and I'm certainly not suggesting in any fashion that they were of a grave moral dilemma. Paul is simply being candid, letting us know that he perceived his service to the Lord as imperfect.

Have you found yourself in that same situation—doing the opposite of what you know God has required of you? As a Christian, loving the Lord God is paramount. We never want to dishonor, shame and hurt our Lord and Savior Jesus Christ. That should always be our overriding motivation for living holy, obedient lives and avoiding sin and disobedient ways.

Yet I had sinned with the very sin I vehemently condemned. There was absolutely no excuse for it. I abhorred, detested, and despised this degradation. Deplorable and unacceptable is the judgment I nailed into myself!

So why am I sharing this story? Why must I debase myself in such a way? The first and foremost reason: My fervent desire is to be devotedly obedient to my heavenly Father, God Almighty. Another reason is that I would like for you, the reader, to know that this author is relating truth from experiencing the depth of God's love personally, not just theoretical notions or church liturgy. Furthermore, we cannot say often enough that anything the devil holds over us and our own lack of devotion creates spiritual weakness. Our prayers for ourselves, not to mention our prayers for others, become diluted and ineffective. God requires us, His children, to purify our consciences from dead works and lifeless observances to serve Him, the living God, fully and unrestrained. In addition, you are loved by the same heavenly Father as I. Perhaps my stupidity (as I look at it now) and my journey of restoration can be an encouragement to you either to avoid worldly wisdom and/or be strengthened through the blood of Jesus throughout your own walk with the Lord. How about you, do you aspire to be holy before the Lord?

Evidently, there must be a world of individuals hiding, suffering from this crippling stronghold of shame yet earnestly desiring to be set free. It's long past the time to clear all roadblocks. The enemy has stopped us in our tracks long enough. God has plans for you and for me. We must be about our Father's business. Let us call upon the Lord to breathe His fresh breath of life and holiness into our dry, decayed, and diseased bones (Ezekiel 37). Even though sin leaves consequences, and the road ahead may be rocky, we repent, move forward without looking back, and stay focused on Jesus Christ.

Surely, David detested his acts of adultery and murder; thus, he repented, "Cast me not away from your presence, and take not your Holy Spirit from me" (Psalms 51:11 ESV). David became one of the mightiest of kings, and God called him a "man after his own heart." Consequences of His sins disrupted his household with one struggle after another for the entirety of his kingship.

Not only David, but the Apostle Paul surely chastised himself for his shortcomings. He called himself "the chief of sinners," an unmerciful murderer of the believers, yet he didn't dwell on the past but looked ahead to serve God fervently whether in personal comfort or not (1 Timothy 1:15; Philippians 3:13-14). It was as if he was making up for his role in the annihilation of the Christians in the early church as well as making up lost time serving God Almighty. Paul, after his conversion, was on a focused mission to further the gospel, just the opposite of his previous Pharisee mind set where he was bent on destroying the gospel. Even when in prison, Paul made good use of the opportunity to share the gospel to the guards and the other inmates and by writing letters of encouragement or correction to the early churches.

In a sense, I feel, in attitude, much the same way as these strong men of God. My devotion to the Lord is rooted and grounded in His *grace* and forgiveness along with knowing firsthand His love for me. My devotion is not based on just mere words of dedication. I know from what I have been saved—that being self-made destruction.

Consider Moses. He was shocked to hear God call his name from a non-consumed burning bush presenting him with an impossible assignment (Exodus 3). Then much later, in doing all to complete the God given assignment, he lost his patience with the ever complaining and murmuring Israelites. Being worn-out emotionally, instead of speaking to the rock as God had directed, regrettably, he angrily struck his staff against the rock—a representation of the Christ yet to come,

which was to bring forth an abundance of thirst-quenching water for the many thousands of people as well as their livestock. You know that had to have been a bitter setback! He'd come so far, he'd accomplished so much with the Lord's help, yet his sin of anger took its toll. Moses was allowed to see the Promised Land only from afar. However, he was still considered "a friend of God" (Numbers 20).

Look at Samson. After years of blindness and destitution, he regained his strength and asked God to trust him one more time (Judges 16). God used him to crush the enemy. Upon pushing against the two major support pillars of the temple with God's enormous imbedded physical strength as well as with the immense spiritual power of prayer, 3000 Philistines died as the temple roof came tumbling down upon them, giving a tremendous victory.

Even Simon Peter, one of Jesus's disciples, was asked three times by Jesus, "Do you love me?"

Of which Peter grieved deeply and replied, "Lord you know all things. You know that I love you" (John 21:13-18).

Jesus replied to Peter, saying, "Feed my sheep."

Peter went on to be the first disciple to proclaim the Gospel on the Day of Pentecost. There were over 3000 conversions, along with the people being filled with the baptism of the Holy Spirit (Acts 2). Peter (*petra*, "a small stone") was also the first to begin taking the Gospel to the Gentiles. He played a prevailing role in the foundation of early Church after Christ's ascension into heaven.

Despite the turn-a-round for the five mighty men of God above, King Saul's story ends in tragedy. He, who had everything a body could ever want or need, started his calling with faith and an attitude of a humble heart. Then, perhaps, as he allowed his position of power to poison his attitude, self-willfulness, claimed him as he impatiently took matters into his own hands one too many times. Sadly, in his pride, he never realized that the spirit of God had left him. He lost everything, including his kingdom, his mental health, his sons, and his own life. (1 Samuel 31).

It seems we, too, have a choice like Saul. We can repent and continue to walk the path God has set out for us, or we can rebel and lose everything. Furthermore, if we remain hidden and cowering in the darkness of strongholds, we continue to sin because we are denying the power of the blood of Jesus. What would have happened historically and spiritually to the Church if these faithful men of God had hidden themselves away under the covering of pride, fear, disgrace, shame, and/or remorse?

May the prayer of Apostle Paul bring to us strength. As you read it aloud, exchange the words "you and us" with your name.

> *For this reason also, since the day we heard this, we haven't stopped praying for you/name. We are asking that you/name may be filled with the knowledge of His will in all wisdom and spiritual understanding, so that you/name may walk worthy of the Lord, fully pleasing to Him, bearing fruit in every good work and growing in the knowledge of God. May you/name be strengthened with all power, according to His glorious might, for all endurance and patience, with joy giving thanks to the Father, who has enabled you/name to share in the saints' inheritance in the light. He has rescued us/name from the domain of darkness and transferred us/name into the kingdom of the Son He loves. We/name have redemption, the forgiveness of sins, in Him (Colossians 1:11-13 HCSB). Amen!*

Although we may feel as though we have sinned with the magnitude of a 10.0 earthquake, if that is conceivable, God continues to look for us to humbly come to Him in repentance. He longs to spread His love and *grace* and mercy upon us. Even though some sin carries a greater consequence; in God's eyes sin is sin. "So, whoever knows the right thing to do and fails to do it, for him it is sin" (James 4:17 ESV). Thankfully, the Bible records the events that clearly display the tragic frailties of mankind. Indeed, it has confirmed the fact that there is nothing new under the sun (Ecclesiastes 1:9). We can learn from these mighty men of history.

God's *grace* and mercy are fully illustrated within the lives of these six great men of God (and others not mentioned), even as the ugly truths of their lives have been exposed. We are privileged to witness not only the detriment of sin, but also the loving forgiveness from God Almighty. We clearly see how He longs for us to persist and continually move forward. He has plans for us (Jerimiah 29:11; Hebrews 10:36;

13:20-21). Undoubtedly, He desires that none should perish and is ever ready to continue loving us, giving us redemption when we earnestly repent—fully turning away from sin. The Lord is the same yesterday, today, and forever (Hebrews 13:8). In other words, what God expected from His chosen ones 2000 years ago, He expects from us today!

Again, why is knowing right from wrong not always enough to keep us from making poor choices? In what ways might you and I be like King Saul? We'll look at several steps that move us into a direction of poor choices in the upcoming chapter, Slippery Slope.

SLIPPERY SLOPE

*A*s WE KNOW, SIN of a shocking nature normally doesn't happen overnight. It's one small step at a time, one poor choice, then another— one undiscerning decision leading us down the path of danger. Or perhaps it's simple carelessness that gets us into trouble. It's a bit like driving on cruise control. We're just coasting down the ribbon of life's merry highway, following the masses without paying attention to or discerning details. When we finally come to our senses, shaking our head, we question, "How in the world did I get here?" We discover we're living in a world of regret and our bed of roses has become a painful bed of thorns. We've become disengaged from our devotion with the Lord and allowed ourselves to be taken captive through the deceptive worldly philosophy of humanistic traditions. Our enemy, Satan, never misses an opportunity to bring even the subtlest temptations our way. He watches. He knows us. He sits and waits for the perfect moment to heap his evil conspiracies upon us.

Furthermore, from our own human nature, even in the most minute measure, the heart pours forth its deceit, pride, and arrogance. Thus, we must be on guard from the depths of our inner most being twenty-four seven. Even the smallest spark of rebellion can derail the heart.

Since sin can slip in on us, how should we be watchful? Quite a number of pastors, evangelists, teachers, and lay people as well, suggest we should constantly be on guard against the enemy's tactics to bring indiscrimination into our walk with the Lord. Beginning with

our attitudes through the measure of our secret place alone with the Lord God Almighty, Lord of Lords and King of Kings, our daily walk requires regular evaluation. Through the numerous questions below, we can meet with the Great Physician. He will highlight our promises and spotlight our areas of need.

One of the first questions we can ask ourselves is, What kind of Christian am I? From within our prayer closet, how fruitful is our time with the Lord in devotion, reading His word, and in prayer? Are our prayers shallow? Perhaps we're spending a lot of effort on an abundance of Christian activities, desiring to be productive in the Kingdom of God and in obedience to the Lord, but these things can also crowd out the personal renewal of private devotions. Are we trusting the Holy Spirit, or do we place more trust in our own understanding?

Psalm 16:11 impresses upon our hearts that God our Father awakens the heart that thrills to the joy of His presence! Spiritually, this is exactly where we want to dwell—in the joy of His presence. Every day is better than the day before. Join with me, won't you, because as we abide in Christ, living close to Him, He provides eternal delights. The joy and intimacy we encounter in our prayer closet forms a protective shield round about us. Our highest call in life is to genuinely love and be deeply acquainted with God following in the footsteps of Jesus Christ (Ephesians 3:14-20 AMP).

In the days of my first marriage, I didn't have a devotional time with the Lord. I didn't have a time carved out for prayer or Bible reading. It was all done haphazardly whenever I was in the mood. When I did sit down to read the Bible, it didn't always make sense to me as I was reading from my own understanding. I didn't know I should ask the Lord to reveal Himself and His thoughts to me while I read. Thus, my spiritual food came from a pastor on a Sunday morning. My main concern, spiritually, was just being a good person and do what seemed right by the standard of what other people thought. I didn't know that the Holy Spirit's role was for each of us today. I had been taught that the Holy Spirit was active only in the people of the New Testament. It wasn't for our modern generation. Subsequently, after I had allowed myself to get involved with another man, I didn't even want to hear the convicting truth of God's word. I was disillusioned with marriage; the sweet attentiveness given outside of marriage had won me over. Thus, I hid behind the lies and carried out the pretentious role of being a good person. Obviously, a protective shield around me or my marriage had not been built securely enough.

Another important consideration revolves around our health and restorative rest. Coming and going, being involved in the Lord's business, counseling, sharing, placing others first are all wonderful as we are called according to the purposes of God. Perhaps our rest is stolen because of an over-scheduled agenda, whether it be of church-related events and activities or of family interests and hobbies such as sports, gymnastics, music lessons, too many appointments or obligations. An overactive lifestyle wears us out and puts undue stress upon us. Possibly, a heavy demand is placed on our bodies due to long work hours in addition to a daily commute. Regardless of what it is, a prolonged hectic schedule can get ahead of us. Without quiet moments and nearness to the Lord, we begin to operate on sheer will power and human thought instead of the guiding light of the Holy Spirit. Eventually, we seek avenues to escape from the pressures of life.

Are you like me in this area? I must watch carefully because it seems I'm never ready to bring closure to the day. I can always find one more seemingly little five-minute thing to do while the clock speeds on towards an hour or more. Thus, I end up trying to make it through the next day by sleeping through the alarm which can cut short my morning devotions just get to work on time. The lack of sleep begins to work to my detriment on my memory, my patience, my attitude, and my mouth. Can you identify?

Hurry hurry rush rush. Are you always chasing about like a roadrunner? Do you find yourself irritated over simple obstacles like the checkout line in your favorite department store for an example, or people in your personal space simply because they're walking slower than you? Maybe traffic seems to move like molasses, and you're moved to road rage! In your absentminded haste you realize too late you ran a red light barely avoiding a crash! You have crucial daily deadlines to meet, and the list goes on and on. Another important question, does your rushed and tired body prevent you from fellowshipping with other Christians or attending church? All of this can create noxious tension. With our hustle and bustle mentality, we may not have suitable time

to process things which can lead us into dismal discernment and poor decisions. Have you forgotten to pray about these situations?

Furthermore, are we easily offended and become overtly offensive? Have we become judgmental and high-minded? I remember being offended by my husband on a regular basis during my first marriage; thus, I was always on the offense. I couldn't seem to duck fast enough when cutting words were slug hitting below the belt.

Are we gossiping through the prayer chain? If our answer is yes, it can be especially dangerous. More recently, I remember the discovery of a breach in privacy after asking a trusted friend to pray with me concerning a stressful personal situation. Overhearing my situation discussed by another individual was most humiliating. It compounded the problem. Not only did I need direction for the stressful situation, I also had to deal with becoming offended and greatly disheartened with those who professed friendship through Christ. It's not just gossip. It's a broken promise; it's lying as well! When we give our word assuring nothing will be repeated, it's best to remember the honor and trust given us by the person in need. Deciding to forgive these well-intentioned individuals was paramount to restoring my heart. Furthermore, they were not intentionally malicious just thoughtless. Perhaps good developed from the ordeal, though, as it demonstrated the necessity to always choose one's comrades with wisdom. In addition, it became a reminder for me personally: be cautious and put a lock on my lips when someone trusts me with their personal information and prayer requests.

More thoughts to consider: Must everything be done to your own standards alone? Do we think of ourselves as little gods, as if we are in control of the universe? Do we act as if God, the great I AM and creator of the universe, is simply a doormat available only to magically do our bidding? Do we have a melt down when God does not perform according to our commands? Have we forgotten to praise the Lord in every circumstance?

No, I didn't praise the Lord in every circumstance during those rough years. I didn't realize I was supposed to give thanks for that husband and those storms of marriage and personality. And, truthfully, if I had known I would most likely have ignored the command (1 Thessalonians 5:18). Any prayers for him were out of self-preservation.

Disparately, I was praying for my husband to die. That's horrible to say from today's perspective, but at the time it seemed fitting. That type of request, I have since learned, is common when a woman feels trapped, and it is more akin to wishful thinking than a prayer. Still, I needed out of the daily despair. I wanted to get beyond that mistake. Asking God to remove him seemed the best way to honorably end the marriage. However, that was not a viable solution. Instead, several years later, the marriage would end through divorce.

Here is another question to consider. Do we have prayer partners or at least one trusted confidant to help hold our hands and heart up within the strength of the Lord, especially during times of weakness? Or, are we only trusting in ourselves? Is the gospel message getting old? Perhaps it doesn't affect our spirit like God intends? Without the fresh eyes and voice of a soul mate, we minimize being held accountable to the journey God has for us. Disaster lurks just around the corner. Beyond the invaluable moments within our prayer closets, the Lord reveals in Matthew 18:20 that "where two or more are gathered in His name, there He is in the midst of them." When we pray according to His Word, He hears our petitions.

Finally, after divorcing, getting resettled, and completing additional education which eventually lead to an excellent employment opportunity, my new spiritual journey began to abound. I was focused on the blessings of Ephesians 3:14-21. The Holy Spirit was actively drawing me into a relationship with the Lord I had never experienced before. Additionally, at this point in my life I had more responsibility than ever. Raising two young children, alone, and starting a demanding job in a distant town caused me to look to the Lord on a new deeper level. As mentioned earlier, the pastor and Sunday School teachers at this church taught that the Holy Spirit was alive, and God's word was active within us. Being captivated, church attendance was where I soaked in the Lord's presence instead of just being present like a good citizen. Here, I found a precious prayer partner friend for a lifetime. What a blessing to share life's challenges through the encouragement of a kindred heart and the power of effectual prayer. Inadvertently, this dear friend also taught me how to pray according to the scripture! I was in love with the Lord and learning to serve Him appropriately. I don't know what changes there might have been in my first marriage if

I would have had such a prayer partner. But, I do know it is imperative to have a friend who will pray sincerely and scripturally with you.

Moving on, another telltale indicator that we could be on a slippery slope has to do with family time. Are we engaging in quality time with our family? Do family members agree with our answers? Building lasting relationships with our God given spouse and children is paramount. How many of our children's events have we missed due to meetings or other obligations? How many community or church activities do we take part in with our family? How many activities do we embrace with our family when we aren't personally interested in their choice of activity? Are our personal interests more important than our family's? Who or what is usurping these precious moments when we neglect them? Are those people or things truly more important than demonstrating our love to our family with our presence? Are we sharing God's goodness with our children? Are we discussing His precepts through the day (Deuteronomy 6:6-7)? Do we have regular family date events that require not just our attendance but our active participation as well? Do we leave our cellphones behind and stay focused on our spouse (if married)? It is said that families help keep our pride in check; they keep us humble.

More questions to help us examine our hearts and to prevent pride from tripping us up. So, in our daily walk with the Lord, what is our motivation for serving Him? Do we make it our goal to be somebody with position? Are we looking for others to lift us up with recognition? Do we get involved in Christian responsibilities so that we can be perceived as righteous and with the need to be exalted? Are we genuinely happy for those growing in the Lord and receiving attention? Are we thrilled when someone repents? Do we pray for their continued victory? Do we readily invite newcomers into our circle of friends and Bible studies? There can be temptation at every corner to be something God never intended for us. Or, are we humble in all the assignments the Lord brings to us? Do we respond quickly to His guidance and direction?

Finally, do we notice sin in the same light as before? Do we continue to be watchful for things that would embarrass our Lord? Does sin continue to concern us, or do we find ourselves quieting our conscience more frequently?

Honestly, for me, the dismal answer was "No." In truth, even though it is difficult for me to admit, my longing to be loved overruled the quiet voice whispering "righteousness." Sin was validated instead of shunned. Even though a phone call would come arranging a meeting place, and knowing I should turn away, I didn't, not for three years. By and by I began to become restless with sinning. It was no longer fulfilling. I desired our relationship to be as a family. My heart began to prefer holiness. I stopped justifying my defiling decisions.

Do we proclaim a modern antidote of "each to their own?" Are we making excuses for or finding it necessary to justify our actions? Do you turn away from offensive language, inappropriate humor, gossip, questionable television programs or sitcoms, scantly clad "news" images? What images do we allow in our home? What images do we allow in our mind's eye? What are we continually thinking or meditating upon? Do we put on the armor of God daily (Ephesians 6:10-18)?

Even though these questions are just as relevant today as they were when I was in my early twenties and newly married, my answer to them, in part, illustrates how the marital problems could continue to escalate. Just about every question would be answered in the negative. Even though I was concerned about wrongs, it was the wrongs in my marriage that mattered most. First off, we were immature. Second, my husband was not a born-again Christian even though he did surrender his life to the Lord much later. Remember, our spirit is changed instantly when we become a believer, but the soul changes, our thinking process, requires us to work out our salvation in obedience to Christ (Philippians 2:12-13). Our third problem was that our pattern of thinking came from the world's ideas around us. Having a weak foundation in Christ, our lives were managed by acceptable social standards. In turn, adopting what was thought to be sophisticated advice to our problematic marriage only served as a springboard for our sin.

We must care! We must have a strong desire to make changes when we recognize we're on a slippery slope. Then, we must be alert to the warning: there will indeed be a heartrending finish line. Remember, the Lord is waiting to hear our cry for His strength. Hold out your hands daily, ask God to fill you with a double blessing of His marvelous *grace*

as He did with apostle Paul (2 Corinthians 12:9). His provision will be sufficient to tirelessly serve Him with excellence of soul.

As David said in Psalm 139:23-24, say aloud, "Search me God, and know my heart: test me and know my anxious thoughts. See if there is any offensive way in me. [If you find anything in me, a thought, a word or any other imagination, cleanse me] and lead me in the way everlasting."

So, what was my excuse all those years ago? These queries seem to be common sense. Looking back, I see a carnal mind-set in both my husband (at that time) and in myself. Christianity—though I believed I loved the Lord—had quiet unspoken political overtones. We, as I see it now, belonged to the denomination of religiosity. We, as husband and wife went to church as good citizens. We went to church to be part of a community and to have a sense of belonging. We went for fellowship with like-minded people. We went to church to receive our kudos. We went to church because it was expected of us. We were full of our own ideas and interpretations following the examples that seemed good to us. We were full of religion, not so full of the spirit of Christ. Reading the Bible seemed necessary and its word important, but rather boring. Since the Bible is a spiritual book, to read with understanding, one needs to read it with the guidance and illumination from the Holy Spirit. If I didn't agree with something or didn't understand, I just skipped over that part. Sadly, I was not in tune with the Holy Spirit. Personal devotions were quick reads, I must admit, that only served to make me feel like I was godly. However, the life in the Spirit was unknown. The vibrancy of living life abundantly was unknown. Also, unknown, especially in the church, was our failing frightful marriage. Perhaps we were more like the Pharisees of the Bible than I'd like to admit.

So, where is our hope of rescue? What responsibility do we have as individuals to know Jesus Christ as our Lord and Savior, as well as our brother? Where do we fit in the overall plan of God? What actions are we taking regarding what we're hearing?

GOD TO THE RESCUE

$\mathscr{B}$ACK MORE THAN 2000 years ago, Jesus Christ, Son of God, came to live on this earth for 33 years. He came to rescue us, His children, from our dark sinful nature. There was a problem, however. Jesus didn't exactly look like or seem to be like God. The people had an entirely different paradigm in mind.

Jesus, in obedience to God the Father, gave up His throne in heaven to clothe himself with flesh, like ours. He, as God the Son, the creator of mankind, became a man Himself, miraculously born of a virgin and laid in a manger—the cattle's food trough as His bed! I'm confident that this stable, a cave, full of livestock, was also rather rank. What a strange way to demonstrate His righteousness, His holiness, His Kingship of heaven! No, we didn't recognize Him as long-awaited king of heaven.

Jesus Christ was born into a family of poverty compared to His heavenly throne. His earthly father figure was a craftsman, a carpenter. He definitely was not what mankind had been looking for as a Messiah! Jesus didn't fit the picture men and women of that era had imagined the Messiah was to be like. Jesus presented himself as a humble servant rather than a man of royalty, prestige, or of military might. His ministry received harsh criticism by the religious leaders. He was mocked, ridiculed, beaten, stripped of clothing, falsely accused, feared, humiliated, tortured, rejected, denounced by the very mankind He was bringing the greatest gifts—salvation, the baptism of the Holy Spirit and fire, and abundant life. (Luke 3:16; John 10:10). His only

crown was one of painful agonizing thorns. He experienced all our pain living as a man, the same that we experience here on this earth. Yet, He was and is the son of God, the Messiah! "Your thoughts are not My thoughts neither are your ways My ways says the Lord; as the heavens are higher than the earth so are My ways" (Isaiah 55:8-9).

Mankind needed a way to become holy because our sins were and are grave indeed! Thus, Jesus Christ freely and lovingly gave everything possible to redeem us. Jesus took our sin, our punishment, and death upon Himself; thus, He exchanged places with us. He gave us eternal life while we give Him our sin, our filthy rags, which deserved the death penalty. He gave His life by dying on the cross at Calvary for our salvation. The law, from the Old Testament, was to be followed in absolute detail; yet man continually broke the law, which served as proof we needed a savior. Jesus, however, lived His life without sin and in constant communion with God the Father. He paid the excruciating price for our salvation by willingly hanging on a rugged cross, dying, going to Hades; and on the third day, He arose as a victor from that odiously dark domain. He had paid a price He did not owe for those He loves because we owed a debt we could never pay. Jesus, therefore, provided the way for us to be adopted as His children into the kingdom of God.

Learning about Jesus and attending summer church camp remain as golden highlights of my childhood. A bonus to the expectations of a glorious camp experience was the route to the camp. Memories of traveling the treacherously narrow curling ribbons of highway along the mountain side are chiseled deeply into my mentality. I could not bear to look out at the immense beauty surrounding us without the feeling of falling off the mountainside! Thus, I hid under a blanket, terrified! I just knew we were goners whenever my uncle would need to downshift while cruising around the numerous hairpin curves! I don't know which brought more relief and gratitude—arriving at camp in all its splendor or getting my feet safely and soundly on the ground! If you've ever traveled the Rocky Mountains, I'm confident you understand.

We especially loved the feel and the novelty of being in the mountains as we were from the broad flatlands, the heart of the breadbasket of the nation. Through the leaders' sensitivity to the

Holy Spirit, our souls were drawn to the creator. Daily cabin center pieces based on various Bible verses were artistically created by the children. Memorized scripture earned us points toward rewards. And cabin inspections revealed who would be holding the duty of kitchen patrol after lunch and dinner. Horseback riding, swimming, hiking, mountain climbing within this backdrop of crisp rugged scenery was exhilarating, especially for an eight-year-old. Now, at the end of a day, a Friday, sitting on a real bear rug during evening services reminded us of choices made by wild critters who became too friendly on the campgrounds. My heart was full and my mind bubbling over with new thoughts, new memories, and new experiences.

Along with my cousin, my older sister and I had been attending this exciting Christian youth camp intricately snuggled into the southern Rocky Mountains for just a couple of years. It was during one of these August camp sessions that Jesus spoke to me in a special way.

During an evening chapel service, my heart with a quickened pace, was heavily pounding within me. A strong warm desire to belong to Jesus filled my soul. As I sat upon that weathered bear rug watching the fervor of the fireplace lap up pinewood as well as pine cones, the Lord tugged at my heart, asking to make Him my home, my Savior. Soon, my turn came to celebrate this new decision.

Shyly, nervously, and with my heart in my throat, I stood. Near the hearth, I took care to choose the finest pinecone from the large open wicker cache. Then turning to the other wide-eyed children eager to hear, I spoke with simple words, "Jesus is my Lord." During a moment above of all moments, I tossed that fragile life into the fire, quickly to be consumed. I had chosen Jesus with sincerity. The old eight-year-old self, like that pinecone, was burned away. The new was just beginning. There would be much to learn.

I would love to say that all my trials, tribulations, and temptations along life's way were met with outstanding victory. However, what I can say is Jesus held my hand through all the trials, tribulations, and especially during major failure with a particularly ardent temptation—all covered by His *grace*. He has brought turning points from rocky roads somewhat like those hairpin curves along a dangerous mountainside. Because of the goodness of the Lord, over the years,

there have been numerous victories far beyond the failures. He has preserved me. Hallelujah! And, He yearns to preserve you as well.

Jesus desires that we continue to exchange our difficulties with Him. We can replace our ashes for His beauty. He wants us to trade our mourning for His oil of joy. He wants to give us His garment of praise if we'll just give Him our spirit of heaviness (Isaiah 61:3). When we surrender our problems, our pain, our confusion, our anger, our failures, our shame, we can move ahead with God's purposes for our lives.

Thankfully, today we have Jesus Christ, who took all our sins upon Himself. He paid for them on the cross, in death, and in His resurrection. He was our blood sacrifice who now intercedes for us at the right hand of God the Father in heaven (Romans 8:34). We are also blessed with the Holy Spirit to lead and direct our steps and our attitude into forgiveness and assist in cleansing our attitudes (John 16:13). Even so, it has not always been this way. Redemption for the sinner came at an exorbitant price! Have you ever wondered how people were forgiven of their sins before the Son of God, Jesus Christ, came?

REDEMPTION: THE WAY IT WAS

$\mathcal{F}$ORGIVENESS. IT COMES THROUGH an inordinately high price! It is only through giving up one's life that the sacrifice becomes operative. Yet it is free to us, the sinner, simply by laying down our lives in repentance before Yahweh, the Lord God Almighty, maker of heaven and earth, King of Kings and Lord of Lords. To fully understand the importance of redemption through the blood of Jesus, come with me to look first at redemption in the Old Testament. Join me as we recognize the wonders of God's plan.

In the Old Testament of the Bible, various types of sacrifices were offered and brought before the Lord God for reconciliation after sin had separated an individual or group from God. Atonement or appeasement for sin was received only after strictly following the numerous facets and details of the law. It was time consuming and messy and could also create a financial hardship. The ceremony had to adhere to the most stringent rules. They were not guidelines, but law to be followed and enforced with precision. Quite honestly, I don't know if I would have been successful following all the rules as required. However, at that time, it was God's provision. It was the way for mankind to come back into a harmonious relationship with Him. There was this one thing though: it required a blood covering. Life had to be given.

Picture this in your mind, if you will: the Holy of Holies. It was the most sacred place within the heart of the tabernacle or temple. The public at large was not permitted to enter this most sacred of all places. This square windowless room is where the Ark of the Covenant,

which represented Israel's relationship with God, was positioned. Only Israel's high priest, and only at a specific time of the year and only after thoroughly cleansing himself during Yom Kippur (otherwise known as the Day of Atonement), could the priest carry the sacrificial blood into the Holy of Holies. He would judiciously present it to God Almighty by sprinkling that blood on the mercy seat of the Ark for the people's atonement as well as for his own sin.

These blood sacrifices were symbolic of the future atonement and forgiveness of sin through Jesus Christ, who would one day, in spirit, cover our sins with His blood from Calvary. The major difference is that, in the Old Testament, the people, on a regular basis, had to select a sacrificial and flawless animal. The animal then gave its life, its blood, for atonement. In other words, the animal's blood became the payment for human sin. Whereas in the New Testament, Jesus Christ, the son of God, was the flawless or sinless sacrifice chosen by our heavenly Father, God Almighty. It was and continues to be the blood of Jesus Christ that covers our sin once and for all—even today and even for all the tomorrows.

Before Jesus the Christ gave up His heavenly throne to come to earth as our savior, it was life-threatening for the people to approach a pure and holy God unless they first had been cleansed from their sin. In Leviticus 20:7, God commanded, "Sanctify yourselves therefore, and be ye holy; for I am Jehovah your God." Sin cannot stand in the presence of God Almighty just like oil cannot mix with water. Therefore, the people followed the precepts of the Law, which required a perfect blood offering to cover their sin. To be cleansed of all their accumulated sins since the last year's Day of Atonement, only the application of a specific unblemished animal's blood could be used. The law powerfully demonstrated the sinful nature of mankind and our need for the Messiah.

Bear with me for a moment while I quickly mention some of the types of sacrifices used by God's people, the Israelites. Looking at the Old Testament sacrifices, even briefly, gives us insight into the beauty of God's gift of our salvation through Jesus Christ. By moving centuries ahead, we know what Jesus has accomplished for us on the cross.

First, the book of Leviticus has illustrated to us that even though there were five basic types of sacrifices, there were also quite a variety of atonement offerings; some were under the category of voluntary and others were mandatory. The people partook in the ones which covered their situation and need. It's important to know there were several reasons other than being sinful that created a need for a person to approach God. Remember, to come before God meant they first had to be consecrated, clean and pure in spirit. Thus, they needed a sacrifice to purify them.

Offering an appropriate sacrifice was the means in which a person could connect with God. Today, we, too, make our connection with the Lord by bringing the sacrifice of praise, and then worship, into the church sanctuary as well as into our own private prayer closet (Hebrews 13:15). As we concentrate on praise and thanksgiving, we cleanse our hearts from daily trials making ourselves ready to receive God's word.

Some of these needs rose out of various daily life activity. Perhaps, for example, they wanted to voluntarily show God their love and devotion through offerings of worship and commitment. Other times, people may have wanted to make a vow in God's presence. Or perhaps someone needed to become ceremonially clean after recovering from a skin disease or giving birth to a child.

There were three voluntary offerings. A voluntary burnt offering or sacrifice was an act of worship to express devotion or commitment to God but also used as an atonement for unintentional sin. Here, a bull, a bird, or a ram without blemish could be used. Only the blood shed for the remission of sin could bring cleansing and purity.

First, there was the voluntary grain or free will offering, as it is sometimes referenced. This unspecified amount of grain sacrifice could be given to God, Yahweh, with frankincense, often following a burnt offering. After meeting various standards, it could be either cooked or uncooked. Even though this offering could not remit sin, the voluntary grain offering was considered the most holy of the food offerings as its purpose was, as an individual, to worship God and acknowledge His provision.

Additionally, drink offerings were followed by both the burnt and grain offering. Here, a specified quantity of wine, dependent upon what animal was being used for the sacrifice, was poured out into the altar fire. The pouring out of a drink offering created a soothing aroma

to the Lord. It is a metaphor for the blood of Jesus literally spilled out from when He was on the cross and when a Roman soldier pierced His side with a spear (John 19:33 NIV). In Luke 22:20 (NIV), Jesus spoke to this when He said, "This cup which is poured out for you is the new covenant in My blood." In 2 Timothy 4:6 (NIV), Paul also uses the phrase when stating, "For I am already being poured out as a drink offering…"

The third voluntary offering was the peace offering, a sacrifice of thanksgiving and fellowship. And, there are offerings that stem off this sacrifice as well, each with its own holy significance.

Perhaps, if we had lived in this day and time as an Israelite, all the sacrifices and means to achieve them would seem perfectly normal as simply a part of life. However, all these laws seem tedious and worrisome to me. They make me feel anxious as if I could never complete them well enough, thus displeasing God, who would have been expecting perfection. Could this be another reason Jesus came to us? It is He who brings true peace within our hearts. It is He who loves us unconditionally.

The two mandatory sacrifices of the Old Testament law had to be fulfilled with precision as well. The first was the sin offering and the other a trespass offering. The sin offering, practiced once a year on the Day of Atonement, was applied for the atonement of sin and to cleanse the people from defilement. The chosen animal used in the sacrifice was dependent upon a person's financial and positional status. A female goat was used by the common person, fine flour was used by the very poor, but a young bull was offered for the high priest and the congregation.

As you can see, these sacrifices all had specific ceremonial rules from the Law requiring they be implemented with excellence. It is interesting to note that the ashes from the sacrifices of atonement were thrown outside the camp. These actions were a precursor to Jesus's death on the cross at Golgotha, also outside the city walls of Jerusalem (John 19:20; Hebrews 13:12). Jewish law did not permit executions and burials inside the city (Golgotha in Aramaic, means: the skull and in Latin, it means Calvary).

The second mandatory sacrifice, the trespass offering, could only utilize a ram for the redemption of unintentional sins that required reimbursement to an offended party, and as a cleansing from defiling sins or physical maladies.

Insomuch that all these sacrifices were used as cleansing and atoning elements, they were flawed. The sacrifices were repetitive due to the sinful nature of mankind. Again, and again, year after year, the people had to bring their sacrifice before the priest for the atonement of their sin whether the sin be intentional or unintentional.

But then Jesus, the Christ, Yeshua, entered the scene. Today we can look back at these sacrifices and view them as a picture of what was to come a few centuries later. All the sacrifices in the Old Testament have pointed toward the perfect and final sacrifice of Christ Jesus, the flawless Lamb of God (John 1:29). As with the rest of the Law, Colossians 2:17 from the New Living Translation tells us that "these rules are only shadows of the reality yet to come. And Christ Himself is that reality." Furthermore, Hebrews 10:1-10 shows us that "we have been made holy through the sacrifice of the body of Jesus Christ once and for all." His death on that old rugged cross opened and invited us into the "holy place, the Holy of Holies" (Hebrews 10:19-23 AMP) so that we can freely enter God's presence and offer our "sacrifice of praise" (Hebrews 13:15; 9:11-28; 4:14-5:10).

Even though we, mankind, still sin, the blood of Jesus will always cover our sin as we come before Him with confession and true repentance. Even today, the command continues, "Be holy, for I am holy" (1 Peter 1:16 KJV). We also learn in Hebrews 9 and 10 that the blood of Jesus Christ, Yeshua, cleanses us, in such an amazing manner that it is as though we had never sinned, leaving us justified—holy. His sacrifice on the cross has done for us what the blood of bulls and goats could never do.

Thankfully so! Jesus Christ believed at the time, as well as today, that you and I are worth His sacrifice. We were worth dying for. We are worth the covering of His *grace*.

JESUS CHRIST, OUR SACRIFICE

*Y*ES, WE ARE WORTH dying for! Isn't that the most amazing reality? In other words, even while I was in the middle of sinfulness, running from the Lord, living life by ungodly standards, He took my sins upon himself, stretched out His arms in love, and welcomed me to Himself. Whenever we surrender in obedience to His invitation of a personal and eternal relationship with Him, the Lord without hesitation, fully welcomes us!

As we hunger and thirst for mercy from our Lord, Yeshua, to cover our sins and bury them in the deepest of seas, remembering them no more, we acknowledge it is only the blood of Jesus that can accomplish forever this incredible covering. Jesus willingly endured and suffered horrifically, signifying the magnitude and depth of His love for all people—for each one of us around the globe—demonstrating His belief that we indeed are worth dying for.

Jesus the Christ desires that we fully understand the lengths He went through so that we could have life everlasting (John 3:16-17). He became the whipping boy or the scapegoat. He took all the punishment we deserved, then set us free as we turn away from sin. Looking fully into His wonderful face, we avail ourselves to receive His glorious *grace*, undeserved favor and forgiveness.

First, as mentioned in the previous chapter, Hebrews 10:4 lauds, "It is impossible for the blood of bulls and goats to take away sins [on a permanent basis]." Animal blood sacrifices had to be repeated yearly; spilling the blood of specific animals, at that time, was the only means in which men and women could compensate for their sin. God, of course, had always been aware of this predicament. When the time was right, He sent His only begotten son, Jesus, as the lamb, the sacrificial lamb, to take away the sins of the world (John 1:29). He would accomplish what could not be done by mere men, the high priests who were the liaisons between God and man and the necessary sacrifices. Full satisfaction of God's requirements for atonement would finally be accomplished (Romans 3:25 AMP).

Jesus confirmed His love for all mankind as He submitted to a criminal's death on our behalf! Not only did He take our condemnation, He also took all our sins (past, present, and future) and shame to the cross, so that we, His children, believers, could live in perfect fellowship and righteousness with Him while on earth now as well as for all eternity. As we know, God presented His Son, Yeshua (Jesus the Christ), as the sacrificial lamb. The time was right. He, Jesus, was the one necessary to blot out the stains of our sins. He covers our sin with His own blood through the cross.

In one of the upcoming chapters, "Come Apply the Blood of Jesus," we will learn more regarding the importance of the blood of Jesus.

Please know that God in all His wisdom and in accordance with His plan of salvation imputed or assigned our sins to be upon Jesus, His only beloved son. Since Jesus Christ was burdened with all our sins, God could now transfer His own righteousness and holiness to us as we repent and turn away from sin. Our action of turning away from sin brings us into a right relationship with both God, our heavenly Father, and with Jesus Christ, the Son of God. In addition, the Holy Spirit releases His power within us to walk in righteousness.

It is important for us to remember that the Word of God in Romans 3:23-26 states *"all* of us have sinned and come short of the glory of God." And in Romans 3:10, "There is no one righteous, not one..." Thus, we *all* need redemption and the power of the Holy Spirit through Jesus Christ. The sacrifice of His blood didn't bring just an atonement, a temporary satisfaction as in the Old Testament, but a once and for all time complete and thorough forgiveness. Through our faith in the blood of Jesus and through the confession with our lips that

Jesus Christ is Lord of Lords, we are redeemed. We are made right with a robe of righteousness covering us (Romans 3:25-26 HCSB).

Additionally, we know the sacrifice Jesus Christ made was excruciating. With the citizens of Jerusalem applauding, He suffered horrific and demeaning barbaric torture as we're about to see.

Can you imagine being an eyewitness to the proceedings of a crucifixion? What about Judas' betrayal of Jesus with a kiss? Would you have been one of those swallowed up within the crowd chanting, "Crucify Him!" "Crucify Him!" repeatedly?

What must Jesus's beloved disciple, His younger cousin, John, have been thinking throughout this whole ordeal? Did he waver in his faith? Was he anticipating Christ to come down off that cross? Or was the entrenched trauma overwhelming and incomprehensible; and thus, he decided not to think but simply follow the instructions of Jesus, "Wait in the Upper Room."?

Jesus's mother, Mary, was there witnessing these traumatically barbaric actions as well. Did she feel the sting within her soul as she heard the snap of each whiplash? Surely, it was heartrending. What must she have thought as she stood at the foot of the cross, looking up at her son? Could it be that she rehearsed all the odd, unusual events and prophesies given since before Jesus's birth—all the things she had pondered and held in her heart (Luke 2:19)? She knew the miraculous conception as stated by the angel, Gabriel. Mary knew her son, Jesus, was born to be the long-awaited-for Messiah. But did she expect to witness Him die a gruesome criminal's death nailed to a cross, so tortured that He was beyond recognition? It seems more than a mother could bear.

Jesus's tribulation begins after the Passover meal and after the first Lord's Supper (communion) while praying in the Garden of Gethsemane. It is written in Luke 22:44, "And being in anguish, he prayed more fervently, and His sweat became like drops of blood falling to the ground" (HCSB).

Have you ever known of anyone to sweat drops of blood? How could this happen? The condition of Hematidrosis is indeed quite rare, so exceptional most people have never heard of it. The condition of Hematidrosis is caused when capillary blood vessels that feed the sweat glands rupture during a time of extremely severe stress or fear, creating a situation where the sweat glands exude blood.

This illustrates just how intense the agony had become for Jesus in His humanity as He accepted the mission God, His Father, had placed before Him. He knew He was about to suffer a most ghastly death, death by hanging on a cross—a type of torture that had been reserved for the most heinous of Roman criminals. Probably, the cross was just one of numerous things on His mind. Perhaps all the other barbaric bloodletting cruelties about to take place at the hands of the Jewish temple leadership and Roman soldiers were flashing through His mentality. Even though His body was about to suffer untold agony and death and be put into the grave, His Spirit would be fully alive. He, Jesus Christ, the offspring of a woman had come to crush Satan (Genesis 3:15). He was about to do battle with Satan himself, along with all the demonic forces of the underworld. Furthermore, He was about to preach His salvation message to all those held prisoner in the realm of the departed (Peter 18:19). Finally, He who knew no sin (2 Corinthians 5:21) was about to be encumbered with all the sins of all the people born to this earth—past, present, and future. Not only this, but in three days, the world would witness God's dynamic, or *dunamis,* power. Jesus would walk right out of the tomb where he was going to be laid. He would rise again fully alive with nail pierced hands and a spear pierced side (Ephesians 1:19-20). Jesus, the Christ, still had more to accomplish in His victory over death (Acts 2:1-41). Certainly, Jesus had much on His mind.

You were on His mind and likewise, I was on His mind as well. Our sin of today, more than two thousand years later, put Him on the cross just as much as the sin of the all the past ages. "Scourging and Crucifixion in Roman Tradition" by William D. Edwards and "The Physician's View of the Crucifixion of Jesus Christ" by C. Truman Davis share why we should profoundly remember this travesty. I pray the Lord will cause us to identify with Jesus and submerge ourselves in the images of His immensely barbaric suffering. I pray it grips our hearts in such a way that we turn away fully in repentance, grieving our sinfulness. I pray it will cause us, with thanksgiving, to love the Lord with our whole heart, soul, mind, and body (Matthew 22:37) and appreciate His *grace* like never before. Oh, what a love Jesus has for us!

After sweating blood in the garden, the second bloodletting came as the officials ripped facial hair out from His face, as referenced from

the Isaiah 50:6 prophecy "I offered my back to those who beat me, my cheeks to those who tore out my beard, I did not hide my face from scorn and spitting..." (HCSB). The offense of beard plucking (to remove violently or abruptly) was accomplished most likely in a heartless manner because Jesus was held captive by those who despised Him. The Jewish officials, along with the Roman cohorts, held only abhorrence for Jesus Christ. The removal of His beard was intended to bring great shame and contempt upon Him because the Bible states, "You shall not shave around the sides of your head, nor shall you disfigure the edges of your beard" (Leviticus 19:27 NKJV). Men were to have a full untrimmed beard in honor of God.

Compounding the pain, the face of Jesus was given a sharp blow. He was slapped by the temple police (John 18:22 and John 19:3 HCSB). Other Bible versions say 'smitten' or struck with rods. Matthew 26:67 from the King James Bible states, "Then did they spit in his face, and buffeted him; and others smote him with the palms of their hands." According to *Merriam-Webster*, "buffeted" is to "drive, force, move, or attack by or as if by repeated blows." Again, He shed more of His precious blood.

John 19:1 has simply and straightforwardly recorded, "Then, Pilate took Jesus and had him flogged."

It pulsates with a jolting image. This scripture—thought to be authored by John, the disciple Jesus loved—need not have additional explanation. Everyone was aware of the gruesomeness of it all. It is extremely overwhelming and unsettling. In fact, you might want to read, if it were possible, with your eyes closed throughout the explanation of what actually took place during the flogging because it's going to get ugly! Initially, a person might think he was just beaten a bit. No, that wasn't the Roman way. He was deeply scourged bringing excruciating pain and shedding of blood as the initial step to being crucified.

Some historians believe scourging, as reported by Williams D. Edwards from the Department of Pathology at the Mayo Clinic in Rochester, Minnesota, in addition to other associates, included a menacing device of judgement—a whip. It was made from the sinews of oxen, and that in it were twisted the hucklebones (ankle or hipbone) of sheep, with sharp slivers of bone and/or small iron balls, in order that every stroke might more effectually tear its way into any criminal's flesh headed for crucifixion. But we're talking about Jesus, who was innocent of all charges leveled against Him. Jesus's flesh was torn away and became progressively more mangled by each horrific blow from the whip!

On a personal note, we all know what it feels like to have a little hangnail torn from a finger. My mind and body cringes at the thought of flesh and muscle being torn away from Jesus's back—as if the soldiers were just tearing scraps of paper. What kept Jesus's mother and all the other followers from running to His rescue screaming, *"stop?"* Surely, their heart's desire was to intervene.

Flogging was a legal preliminary to every Roman execution. For scourging or flogging, the man was stripped of his clothing, and his hands were tied to an upright post. The back, buttocks, and legs were flogged either by two soldiers (lictors) or by one who alternated positions. The severity of the scourging depended on the disposition of the soldiers and was intended to weaken the victim to a state just short of collapse or death. As the Roman soldiers repeatedly struck the victim's back (up to thirty-nine times) with full force, the iron balls would cause deep contusions, and the leather thongs and sheep bones would cut into the skin and subcutaneous tissues. Then as the flogging continued, the lacerations would tear into the underlying skeletal muscles and produce quivering ribbons of bleeding flesh. Pain and blood loss generally set the stage for circulatory shock. A prophesy foreshadowing Jesus's unjust punishment before his death, grievously states, "Plowmen have plowed my back and made their furrows long" (Psalm 129:3).

As if this agony was not enough compounded suffering, a scoffing company of about two hundred Roman soldiers surrounded Jesus and affixed a crown of thorns upon His head and then proceeded to use a staff to strike Him upon His head again and again (Matthew 27:27-31). The crown of thorns most likely came from a plant like the Aramaic *Nubk* plant, which has long spinney sharp nail like thorns and was plentiful in the Jerusalem vicinity. Both pain and blood resulted as the platted vine was pressed and fitted into His head.

Following the torment of the crown of thorns, the soldiers led Jesus off to be nailed to His cross (John 19:17-19 HCSB). Blood was

again shed as nails, more like long spikes, were driven into His wrists (the wrist is considered part of the hand), which severed the median nerve, creating additional severe pain and blood loss as well as paralysis of the hands. His feet, placed one atop of the other, were also nailed to the cross shedding even more blood.

The final loss of blood as well as water took place at the ninth hour, which is 3:00 p.m., after Jesus shouted out in a loud voice (Matthew 27:50), "It is finished!" (John 19:30 HCSB). After the officers noticed that Jesus had already expired, they did not break His legs. But they thrust a spear up into His side which released much blood and water (John 19:34; Psalm 22:14-15).

The blood of Jesus and His death are not as simple of a matter as often thought. Have you been able to grasp the teachings of the complexity and depth of Jesus's suffering? The full affect had not penetrated my heart and mind until writing this ghastly description.

Discussing this gruesome loss of blood seems to accentuate the price Jesus paid for our forgiveness, His grace and love on full display. He suffered the letting of His precious blood in eight different ways during the process of being crucified. He gave to us everything when He gave His life as a sacrifice. I believe He told us and continues through the Word to tell us that we, each one of us on this earth, are the purpose for His suffering, His ministry of the cross, and beyond. Jesus Christ is a love like no other! Regardless of what our sin/s have been or are, He loves us deeply. There has not been a sin created by man that He has not already forgiven at Calvary and continues to forgive when we repent. Jesus even forgave His barbaric abusers while He was still in agony hanging on the cross (Luke 23:34)!

Truly, I believe, receiving forgiveness from the Lord is the simple, uncomplicated part of our battle for freedom from the condemnation of our sin. For us, we only need to confess our sin and freely receive what Christ has freely given.

The tough part may be dealing with the memories or the woundedness of our soul, which continues to linger along with accusations. These seem to be the things we must work out after receiving forgiveness. It has been for me. Obtaining victory over the guilt and shame Satan puts on us is imperative. The blood of Jesus paid it all.

REMEMBER NO MORE

*H*ALLELUJAH! AS CHRISTIANS, WE know we have been redeemed, bought back, or purchased again by the blood of the lamb, Jesus Christ. For Romans 10:9 states, and I say again as in past chapters, "If you declare with your mouth, 'Jesus is Lord,' and believe in your heart that God raised him from the dead, you will be saved." But, do you know that "God forgives and remembers our wickedness no more" (Hebrews 8:12)?

Often, relentless guilt and harrowing shame laid on us by the accuser, Satan, will hinder us from believing that we have indeed been redeemed into the kingdom of God through the shed blood of Jesus Christ. As a Christian, after reverting into sinfulness, the same is true. Our adversary loves to fill our mind with his lies, causing us to think and feel as though we have not been liberated from the sting of our sinfulness. Shame and fear of disgrace can cause us to become lame and fearful because our eyes are seemingly superglued onto the past with self-condemnation much like being preoccupied by a tiny dark smudge on an otherwise spotless white shirt.

Thus, we cower and are held hostage instead of taking advantage of our freedom in Christ. We might continue to believe and perceive our sin to be too abhorrent and detestable, thus hide from serving the Lord by staying under the darkness of additional self-imposed guilt. Our pride forbids us to openly admit to ourselves, let alone others, that we have committed the unthinkable; so we put on a face of virtue, attempting to ignore our crime as well as its ramifications. More

protectively, we absolutely run from anyone or anything that might condemn us or point their finger magnifying our shame—whether privately behind our backs or worse, announce our shame publicly.

There is another side to the coin. What we have done, hiding in guilt, has given the enemy free reign to hold us captive, crippled, and in bondage. Even though our sin may have been an appalling abomination as well as being greatly humiliating to us and others, we must allow the Lord to remove our fear and our *'stinkin thinkin'*. It is imperative that we allow ourselves to receive His compassionate love, His *grace*, and forgiveness of both sin and guilt.

It is incredibly important to stop measuring ourselves against the past. When we repent, God does forgive us; in fact, He disregards our dirty deed by placing it under the blood of Jesus. We must start to act on God's word. He is with us! Jesus Christ, our Lord, will run with us to finish the race He has set before us. Hiding in our guilt, as I have done for years, continually grieves the Lord! Whether we purpose to or not, the hiding causes us to continue in sin because we are ignoring God's provisions as well as not believing Him to be faithful to His own word. "It is I who sweep away your transgressions for My own sake and remember your sins no more" (Isaiah 43:25, Jeremiah 31:34). If God does not remember our sin, why do we? What can we do?

Together, let us take the bold step of applying the blood of Jesus and looking at the scriptures and reading them aloud, replacing any pronouns with your name, decreeing and declaring God's Word to be effective within the depths of our being. Job 22:28 explains that when we decree a thing, it shall be established unto you. It is through our words, our testimony, and confession of scripture that we overcome and break free from the throes of self in addition to our enemy, the devil. Jesus paid too great a price for us to deny the truth and power of His blood sacrifice. Let us run into the cleft of the rock, Jesus Christ, who brings us our victory!

COME, APPLY
THE BLOOD OF JESUS

$\mathcal{W}$E CAN APPLY THE life blood of Jesus, personally, to our own lives in much the same way the blood was applied to the doorposts of the Jewish homes in the days of Moses. Remember the Biblical account of the great plagues of Egypt? Moses was sent by God to convince Pharaoh to let His people, the Jewish slaves, leave Egypt and be set free from their bondage. God had brought nine horrible plagues upon all of Egypt due to Pharaoh's stubborn refusal to release the Israelite slaves. Before the tenth and final plague, the death of the first born, a hyssop branch (a type of herbaceous weed like plant) was utilized like a paint brush to apply the blood of an unblemished sacrificial lamb upon the doorpost of each Jewish home. When the death angel from God came that night, it passed over these homes, leaving the occupants of the house safe and untouched by death. These individuals were saved from death because they had been obedient to God's instructions by staying under the covering of the blood. Derek Prince, in *How to Apply the Blood* states, "We apply the blood of Jesus as with a hyssop branch—with our own spoken words" (Used by permission of Derek Prince International. Inc; www.derekprince.org). Similarly, in Psalms 51:7, David implores the Lord to "cleanse me with hyssop, and I will be clean; wash me, and I will be whiter than snow." Both the blood of Jesus and the Word of God are extremely powerful!

The following nine ways in which the blood of Jesus affects our lives brings more than cleansing alone. The blood of Jesus also brings healing to our spirit, body, and soul. When we place the words of God Almighty deep into our spirit and soul, we become strengthened with preparation in our warfare against the devil and all his inflictions against us. In addition, it enables us to hold our head up high above any shame we may be feeling. Consequently, let us remember to personalize the following scriptures as we purposefully slip them into our spirit, fully grasping the power in the blood of Jesus Christ. Remember, we can determine the course of our lives by the words that we speak!

We'll visit nine aspects in which the blood of Jesus not only divinely touches us but touches in a glorious manner. Hallelujah! Our Lord is immensely good to us!

The blood of Jesus has brought to us *redemption*.
The blood of Jesus has *cleansed* us.
The blood of Jesus has *justified* or declared us as being not guilty.
The blood of Jesus has *sanctified* us.
The blood of Jesus has given us new *life*.
The blood of Jesus *intercedes* on our behalf.
Through the blood of Jesus, we have *access* to our heavenly Father.
The blood of Jesus brings to us *power* through the Holy Spirit.
The blood of Jesus *seals* our place in the Kingdom of God.

The blood of Jesus has *redeemed* us!

"Therefore, there is now no condemnation for those who are in Christ Jesus, because through Christ Jesus the law of the Spirit who gives life has set you free from the law of sin and death" (Romans 8:1). Through His shed blood, Jesus Christ has bought us back. As an example of personalizing or replacing the pronouns with your name, you could read Romans 8:1 like this: Therefore, there is now no condemnation for me, *[your name]*, because I am in Christ Jesus. Because through Christ Jesus, the law of the Spirit who gives life has set me, *[your name]*, free from the law of sin and death. Remember, as we participate in engraving the scripture within our spiritual being, the Holy Spirit begins His work ever so deeply within our soul. Ephesians 1:7 also states "In Him we *[your name]*, have redemption through His blood, the forgiveness of sins, in accordance with the riches of God's grace." In addition, "[God] hath delivered us, [*your name*], from the power of darkness and hath translated us, [*your name*], into the kingdom of his dear Son" (Colossians 1:13 KJV). Therefore, let us say so! It is a must! Hallelujah! Remember, It is through the blood of the lamb and the word of our testimony that we triumph over Satan (Revelation 12:11).

When we speak God's truth aloud, our spirit is more attentive and believes more dearly, therefore we say: "*I decree and declare, 'Through the Blood of Jesus, I have been redeemed out of the hand of Satan including all of his scheming spiritual forces of darkness.*'" (Used by permission of Derek Prince International, Inc. <u>www.derekprince.org</u>).

We are *cleansed* by the blood of Jesus!

In John 8:12, Jesus refers to Himself as "the light of the world." "But if we walk in the light, as he is in the light, we have fellowship with one another, and the blood of Jesus, his Son, purifies us from all sin" (1 John 1:7). "If"—what a momentous word! It requires us to be actively engaged. As Derek Prince and other teachers of the Word have taught, we must continually walk and have fellowship with the light, so that God's glory light, Jesus Christ, can continue to cleanse us from sin. Walking in the light is evidenced by being in fellowship with Jesus. If we are not in fellowship; then neither are we in the light. Sin can only be cleansed in and by the light. Nevertheless, the light of Glory responds instantly when we surrender our sin to Him. The blood washes us white as snow (Psalm 51:7). Thankfully, the Holy Spirit continually works within us to draw us unto repentance and away from sin as well.

Apply the blood of Jesus by stating aloud: "*On the authority of God's word, I declare and decree, 'While I walk in the light, the blood of Jesus cleanses me now, this very moment, from all my sin.*'" (Used by permission of Derek Prince International, Inc. www.derekprince.org).

We are *justified* by the blood of Jesus!

"Since we have now been justified by his blood, how much more shall we be saved from God's wrath through him" (Romans 5:9)! Being justified is being treated as righteous. Jesus has made us righteous through His own righteousness (2 Corinthians 5:21). His blood has

acquitted us—declared us not guilty. It is as if we had never sinned! Romans 10:10 continues, "For it is with your heart that you believe and are justified, and it is with your mouth that you profess your faith and are saved." We could never cleanse or justify ourselves because Isaiah 64:6 (NLT) says, "We are all infected and impure with sin. When we display our righteous deeds, they are nothing but filthy rags..." Then, in Romans 4:24-25, we read, "He [Jesus] was given over because of our transgressions and was raised for the sake of our justification." Psalm 103:12 continues, "as far as the east is from the west, so far has he removed our transgressions from us." In addition, from Micah 7:19, we can understand that our sins are buried in the depths of the sea, never to be remembered.

Let me say again that our forgiven sin will never bring God's penalty of wrath or condemnation! Our sin has been blotted out of His memory. "Blessed are those whose transgressions are forgiven, whose sins are covered. Blessed is the one whose sin the Lord will never count against him" (Romans 4:7-8). We are blessed! Hallelujah! Isaiah 61:10 (HCSB) beautifully leads us to this joyous exclamation, "I greatly rejoice in the LORD, I exult in my God; for He has clothed me with the garments of salvation and wrapped me in a robe of righteousness...!" Yes indeed, we have been justified!

Apply the blood of Jesus by stating: *"I decree it to be true and declare with my mouth, 'Through the blood of Jesus, I am justified, acquitted, not guilty, reckoned righteous, and made righteous just as if I had never sinned.'"* (Used by permission of Derek Prince International, Inc. www.derekprince.org). Amen!

We are *sanctified* by the blood of Jesus!
Scripture illuminates God's desire that we be sanctified, made saintly, made holy, without spot or wrinkle, and set apart to do His will. The following three verses clearly illustrate that through Christ Jesus, as His children believing upon Him, we become sanctified: "Therefore, Jesus also suffered outside the gate, so that He might sanctify the people by His own blood" (Hebrews 13:12 HCSB). "Yet now he [God] has reconciled you to himself through the death of Christ in his physical body. As a result, he [God] has brought you into his own presence, and you are holy and blameless as you stand before

him without a single fault" (Colossians 1:22 NLT). "By this will of God, we have been sanctified through the offering of the body of Jesus Christ once and for all" (Hebrews 10:10 HCSB).

Sanctification is a work which God performs, as an intricate part of our salvation, our commitment, and connection with Christ (Hebrews 10:10). You may be thinking, "But I could never be holy. Only God can be holy." Yet, even though our sin may be crimson red, remember our confessed sin is under the blood of Jesus, forgotten.

Besides that, being holy is not something that one feels. At least, I have never felt holy. Instead, it is in the simple truth of God's word. We are made holy through Christ Jesus. We can accept it, however, as part of God's gracious gift that He so lovingly bestows within us. It certainly isn't through anything we have done; it's what Christ has done on our behalf. It is a humble state of being as a follower of the Lord Jesus Christ.

Apply the blood of Jesus by stating aloud, *"I decree and declare, 'Through the blood of Jesus, I am sanctified, made holy, set apart to God, separated from sin, and made holy with God's holiness.'"* (Used by permission of Derek Prince International, Inc. www.derekprince.org).

We have been given *life* through the blood of Jesus!

The Bible speaks of God's life, the life of Jesus, and the life given by the Holy Spirit by various means. Sometimes it is life given with faith in our salvation; other times, it is given as we in faith, believe. Still again, it is given in faith through partaking of the Last Supper. All our spiritual life flows through our faith. The following three scriptures substantiate this thought (remember to continue to personalize the scriptures by exchanging the pronouns as appropriate with your name): "In the beginning was the Word, and the Word was with God and the Word was God; in him was life, and that life was the light of all mankind. The Word became flesh and made His dwelling among us" (John 1:1-4, 14). "For the life of the flesh is in the blood, and I have given it to you on the altar to make atonement for your souls; for it is the blood that makes atonement, by reason of the life [which it represents]" (Leviticus 17:11 AMP). Christ Jesus said, "Very truly I tell you, the one who believes has eternal life. I am the bread of life. I am the living bread that came down from heaven. Whoever eats this bread

will live forever. This bread is my flesh, which I give for the life of the world" (John 6:47-51).

Even though they did not understand, Jesus again told the crowds, "Very truly I tell you, unless you eat the flesh of the Son of Man and drink his blood, you have no life in you" (John 6:53). The people thought Jesus was talking about physically eating his human flesh. No, He was speaking allegorically (with hidden meaning); it is as if we bite into the truth of God's Word like we bite into a slice of tasty bread or meat (flesh/bread/Jesus), we chew on it; we meditate upon it, and we receive its meaning into our hungry spirit, resulting in spiritual growth. We receive His life within our spirit, and that holy life then overflows into our physical body.

The second half of Jesus's statement, "and drink his blood" was also greatly disturbing to the religious leaders and thus to the people. They rebelled against the repugnant thought of drinking blood because it was forbidden by the law. But again, Jesus was not speaking in literal terms. His blood equated life. The people only had to believe. At the Passover Meal as the Last Supper (now often referred to as "communion") the cup or the new wine was presented. It symbolized the life of Christ and his teachings, in addition to the blood He was about to shed. Furthermore, Jesus taught, "This cup is the new covenant in my blood, do this, whenever you drink it, in remembrance of me" (1 Corinthians 11:25).

So the life of God is in the blood of Jesus. And Jesus tells us in John 10:10 that He came to earth to give us life—not just a life, but an abundant life! Continuing, Jesus said in John 6:63 that it is "the Holy Spirit [the third person in the Trinity—God the Father, God the Son, and God the Holy Spirit] that gives life, the flesh counts for nothing, the words I have spoken to you are full of the Spirit and life." Again, we may not fully grasp all the concepts concerning the mysteries of life spoken of by Jesus. However, from Ephesians 3:20 (AMP), we learn just how miraculously magnificent our God is. For He "is able to [carry out His purpose and] do superabundantly more than all that we dare ask or think [infinitely beyond our greatest prayers, hopes, or dreams], according to His power that is at work within us." The life of the creator, God, is infinitely greater than we, the created. Since we are created in the image of God, we have a special place within our being for His spirit to reside, which gives us life in Christ (1 Corinthians 6:19 NIV). 'Don't you know that you yourselves are God's temple and that God's Spirit dwells in your midst?" (1 Corinthians 3:16). This special place is the temple of God.

Here are just a few examples demonstrating God's creativeness being infinitely greater than anything you or I could possibly create. And to think, this same power of God's spirit resides within us as Christians.

First, examine the heavenlies and consider the one or maybe two trillion galaxies, according to a 2016 CBS report, that make up our universe! Imagine, our earth's galaxy, the Milky Way, is just a tiny drop in the bucket! Is that not mind boggling?

Furthermore, consider the magnificent grandeur in the silent splendor of the evening sunset and the majesty of the morning's sunrise. Both are absolutely too phenomenal for any human to envision, let alone create!

Next, behold the mystifying and secluded nine-month journey of a preborn baby in addition to his or her loud exclamation, along with that first breath of fresh air.

Lastly, explore the delicacies of a tender blossom and its fragrance spilling over, inviting us to examine closely as it miraculously unfolds its fragile petals in exquisite finery. All these events of life are perfectly precise at the command of God's quiet whisper.

"Oh, how great are God's riches and wisdom and knowledge! How impossible it is for us to understand His decisions and His ways! For who can know the Lord's thoughts? Who knows enough to give him advice? And who has given him so much that he needs to pay it back? For everything comes from him and exists by his power and is intended for his glory. All glory to him forever! Amen" (Romans 11:33-36 NLT). Great is Yahweh our God! Life! The cosmos, the earth, and us—we are made alive with the life of Christ spoken into existence by the word of God!

Again, we apply the blood of Jesus by faith. Humbly and prayerfully declare, *"Lord Jesus, when I receive your blood, in it I receive your life—the life of God, divine eternal endless life. Thank you, Lord."* Tenderly receive it; pause and let the sense of divine life fill you right now, your heart, even your body." (Used by permission of Derek Prince International, Inc. www.derekprince.org).

The blood of Jesus *intercedes* for us.

The author of Hebrews 12:22-24 reminds us that we as Christians "have not come to the mountain of fear, darkness, and gloom. Instead we come to Mount Zion!" Within Mount Zion we come to seven marvelous greetings.

Among these greetings, we come to Jesus, the mediator of a new covenant, and to the sprinkled blood of Jesus, which He willingly gave. It continues to speak for mercy on our behalf and is always interceding for us. Romans 8:34 confirms that Jesus sits at the right hand of God the Father interceding—bringing our requests along with our brokenness, to the throne of God the Father.

With certainty, His intercession is always genuine and effectual. Thankfully, the Holy Spirit was guarding over me during an extremely difficult time of shock and disbelief. As shared in my first book, *Jesus, A Love Like No Other!*, while grieving the loss of Ken, my second husband of 19 years, I was feeling immensely defeated, weary, confused, and alienated from the living. It was then that a blackness crept into my mind and began to fill it in with absolute absence of any hint of light, becoming pitch black. Like a clock, on every quarter hour, the darkness grew to be about three-quarters complete within my mind. I could not think, let alone know what it was. I could feel, however, that I was ready to surrender to its presence. The blackness beckoned and coaxed me to simply slip away into its comfort of carelessness and hollow darkness. I was more than willing to enter that pit of nothingness. Simultaneously, with my mentality fully engaged within this scene, came the voice of authority, the Holy Spirit, from deep within my hearing; a sudden loud shout commanded, "No!" Like a popped balloon, the blackness vanished, totally gone; and just like that, I returned to my senses. I had no thought to pray, nor could I pray. Most likely the blackness, I believe to be authored by Satan, was an invitation to enter deeply rooted depression or some other state of mental illness separating me from reality. Forever grateful, through the blood of Jesus, the ever-watchful Holy Spirit had interceded on my behalf. Hallelujah!

We may apply the blood of Jesus by decreeing and declaring our gratitude,

"Thank you, Lord, that my prayers and even when I cannot pray, the blood of Jesus is pleading or interceding for me in heaven" (Used by permission of Derek Prince International, Inc. www.derekprince.org).

We have *access* to the Father through the blood of Jesus!

The author of Hebrews 10:19-24 strongly encourages us to enter the most holy place by the blood of Jesus boldly and confidently. A new and living way has been opened for us through the torn curtain that is his body, into the eternal heavenly realm. While Christ was alive, the veil or curtain hanging between the holy place and the most holy place was a symbol of separation. No one could enter the most holy place except the high priest and then only on the Day of Atonement. We were separated from God. But at Christ's death on the cross, this very same temple curtain was ripped from top to bottom. Some Bible historians believe this temple curtain was about 60 feet in height and about four inches thick. Amazing! Regardless of the dimensions, it removed the barrier that had prevented mankind from having a personal relationship with God and symbolized our new freedom of access into the *holy of holies.*

Since we have in Jesus Christ a great high priest over the house of God, let us draw close to Him with a sincere heart and with the full assurance that faith brings. Our hearts are sprinkled to cleanse us from a guilty conscience. Our bodies are washed with pure water. Let us hold unswervingly to the hope we profess, for he who promised is faithful. We hold fast to our words of confession that Jesus Christ is Lord of all. Even in the most daunting of times, let us continually hold our confession appropriately focused on God's truth, trusting always in Him. His words are life to those who find them (Prov. 4:22). We overcome Satan, our adversary, by the blood of Jesus and the word of our testimony. Jesus welcomes us into the throne room of God where we access victory! Through Jesus Christ we have direct access to God our Father—not just access, but a welcoming access. God bids us to come to Him.

State aloud, *"Thank you Lord that through the spilt blood of Jesus, I have access into your presence, into the holiest place in the universe"* (Used by permission of Derek Prince International, Inc. www.derekprince.org). Amen.

We have *power* through the blood of Jesus!

The Word of God describes the necessity for believers to be filled with the power of the Lord. This power, the Holy Spirit, was given

through the blood of Jesus Christ after His resurrection. One reason we need to be empowered is to complete the work God has set out for us, His people, His masterpieces. The Amplified Bible states that we are reborn from above—spiritually transformed, renewed, ready to be used for good works, which God prepared for us beforehand, taking paths which He set so that we would walk in them, living the good life which He prearranged and made ready for us (Ephesians 2:10). In Acts 1:5, the apostle Paul records the words of Jesus, specifically saying, "For John baptized with water, but you will be baptized and empowered and united with the Holy Spirit, not long from now."

Next, our need for power comes in Acts 1:8 as it continues to clearly direct us, "But you will receive power and ability when the Holy Spirit comes upon you; and you will be My witnesses [to tell people about Me] both in Jerusalem and in all Judea, and Samaria, and even to the ends of the earth." Thus, we need power to preach the word of God to all the nations and power to be witnesses.

Third, we need the power of the Holy Spirit for us to be like Jesus and do even greater things than Him. John 14:12 (AMP) expounds by repeating Jesus's words: "I assure you and most solemnly say to you, anyone who believes in Me [as Savior] will also do the things that I do; and he will do even greater things than these [in extent and outreach], because I am going to the Father."

Why do we need power? Because in our daily walk, spiritual battles rage. The enemy comes to destroy. He despises and loathes the believers of Christ. He loves devastation and loves to create failures for God's children in every magnitude. As described in Ephesians 6:12 (AMP), "we are not wrestling with flesh and blood [contending only with physical opponents], but against the despotisms, against the powers, against [the master spirits who are] the world rulers of this present darkness, against the spirit forces of wickedness in the heavenly (supernatural) sphere." However, with the power of the Holy Spirit we are more than conquerors—we are victorious! "Then I heard a loud voice in heaven, saying, the accuser... has been thrown down [at last], he who accuses them and keeps bringing charges [of sinful behavior] against them before our God day and night. And they overcame and conquered him because of the blood of the Lamb and because of the word of their testimony" (Revelation 12:10-11).

This power also gives us the ability to love the Lord with our whole mind, spirit, and body. We can fulfill John 14:15, "If you love me, you will keep my commandments." when we are truly surrendered to the Lord. The power of the Holy Spirit assists us mightily.

Let us abide in the presence of the Lord and receive with open hearts His promised power. Ask the Lord to fulfill His promise in you and believe through faith that He has. Pray aloud, *"Lord, clothe me with your power, your Holy Spirit, so that I can live victoriously moment by moment as I run the race you have set before me. In Jesus's name, Amen."*

We are *sealed* belonging to Him through the blood of Jesus.

"And you also were included in Christ when you heard the message of truth, the gospel of your salvation. When you believed, you were marked in him with a seal, the promised Holy Spirit" (Ephesians 1:13). It is a seal, a guarantee, that can never be broken. Even when a child of God sins, grieving the Holy Spirit, the seal remains. It is permanent because we have been purchased by the life blood of Jesus. It is His blood that has preserved us with an unperceivable mark, avowing to the entire spirit world that we who declare with our lips and believe in our hearts that Jesus Christ is Lord do indeed belong to Jesus Christ. Nothing can remove us from the hand of God Almighty. The Apostle Paul, being fully convinced of this very thing, teaches us "that neither death nor life, neither angels nor demons, neither the present nor the future, nor any powers, neither height nor depth, nor anything else in all creation, will be able to separate us from the love of God that is in Christ Jesus our Lord" (Romans 8:38-39). We have heard the testimony of Jesus Christ in John 10:28. Christ, Himself, has testified "I give them eternal life, and they shall never perish; no one will snatch them out of my hand."

Therefore, let us joyously decree and declare, *"Thank you Lord. Through your salvation, your sprinkled blood has placed the precious mark of the Holy Spirit upon me, sealing me, preserving me for all eternity in the Kingdom of God. You are Lord of Lord's and King of Kings, God Jehovah, God Almighty, the Great I AM! Hallelujah!"*

Through the faith in the blood of Christ Jesus, God has provided us with *redemption, cleansing, justification, sanctification, life, intercession, access,* and *power.* Furthermore, He has *sealed* us as His for all eternity. Is any one of these benefits of more importance than another? Of course not, it's a package deal. "Cause us, Lord, to remember all your benefits" (Psalm 103). The blood of Jesus is all in all. The blood of Jesus has made it possible for us to come straight into the holy of holies dwelling in and with the Lord's presence. No longer must we present a sacrifice of a prescribed animal or grain offering. Rather, we bring ourselves humbly. We are free to come to Jesus Christ just as we are—in our frail humanity. Instead of placing His judgement upon us, He welcomes us with love, mercy, and *grace.* Jesus says, "Come close and I will come close to you" (James 4:8 NLT).

Should it be that you are struggling with receiving freedom from condemnation because of past sin, consider recording and memorizing the nine applications of the blood of Jesus Christ. Then when the enemy comes to bombard you with his accusations, you will be prepared to send him packing. You will be prepared for victory as you confess what the Word of God states. Miracles take place when we speak God's Word. It transforms us more completely into His image, where the spirits of shame and remorse never live.

As one of the 19th-century fathers of the faith, revivalist, evangelist, pastor, and one of the best-loved and most widely read writers on faith and spirit-filled living, Andrew Murray, has written and recorded in chapter two of his on-line book, *The Power of the Blood of Jesus,* "Shelter under the ever-continuing sprinkling of the blood. Ask the Lamb of God Himself to make the blood efficacious in you. You will surely experience that there is nothing to compare with the wonderworking power of the blood of Jesus."

Hallelujah! Faith, forgiveness, and a clean heart are products of the Lord He so joyfully instills in us.

Now, what do we do with the woundedness created by sin. Let's look at encountering further healing and discovering the value of God's *dunamis* power when applied to our wounded soul.

OUR WOUNDED SOUL

$\mathcal{S}$IN, OFFENSES, AND/OR TRAUMA of any kind can create profound crippling soul wounds deeply seated within our beings. Even after confessing our sin to the Lord and being completely forgiven, whether the wickedness was by our own choice or a wrong committed by others done to us, that sin can invite and allow woundedness, raw and bleeding, to form within our soul.

Sometimes the soul is referred to as our heart; it's the rational or psychological part of our being and is composed of our mind, will, and emotions. Woundedness within our soul is like a collection of unrecognized anger, anguish, hostility, grief, regret, shame, unforgiveness, and heartache, to mention just a few issues. Pain from woundedness harbors within our being and can create enormous mental, physical, and spiritual dilemmas for us.

In other words, our soul can accumulate a lot of gunk if we're not watchful. It's a bit like a classy little coupe` that gradually develops various conditions of coughing, sputtering, moaning, groaning, and whining as it goes down life's road. The engine, power steering, and its gas line have become clogged with sticky goo and mire. Renovation by a certified mechanic to recalibrate and fine-tune this gem is imperative! Like the coupe, we need to allow the Holy Spirit to bring our wounded soul into proper calibration with the Word of God.

Again, even though we have asked the Lord for forgiveness and have been thoroughly forgiven, that woundedness created by the sin must be dealt with; or it will linger in the depths of our soul. If left

unattended, it will continue to fester within us. All sin is corrosive to our relationship with the Lord. The wound unbolts doors and welcomes our accuser, the devil, to create additional havoc. He will not miss an opportunity to take full advantage of us because he roams the earth looking for those he may devour (1 Peter 5:8).

Having a wounded soul is certainly not a new phenomenon. Wherever there is emotional difficulty, stressful struggles, grievous illnesses or offenses, most likely we humans have been wounded in the process. One example is with Cain and Able from the very first book of the Bible, Genesis.

In Genesis 4, we are shown the plight of taking offense. Cain was deeply offended because God did not accept his sacrifice. He became indignant, hostile, and angry with God, in addition to being jealous of his brother, Able, whose sacrifice God had accepted. Even though the Lord told Cain that if he would do what was acceptable and pleasing, he, too would do well. Then God warned and instructed Cain to master the sin crouching at his door. Sadly, Cain seemed to be on a different course. He allowed his wounded soul to fester until he lashed out, killing his brother! Cain had been inundated with unrelenting woundedness from offense, his jealousy, which was demonstrated by his attitude and reactions.

A second example is with Job. He was wounded as well by the trauma of sudden loss of his family members, disaster, and horrific health issues. In addition, his friends blamed Job for his plight. Their consolation and accusations only caused his affliction to become more deeply imbedded. They believed that Job, their friend, was hiding sin. They believed all the turmoil was his punishment. Amid all the struggle and even though Job continued to worship the Lord saying, "The Lord gave and the Lord has taken away, blessed be the name of the Lord" (Job 1:21 ESV), he is in shock. His woundedness caused him to speak out in "bitterness *of his soul*"; he despised and loathed his own life (Job 10:1). [Even though Job while in severe turmoil spoke against his own life, the Bible tells us that he did not sin against God!] There is a happy ending to Job's life. God restored all that had been taken away and multiplied blessings to him because Job had remained ever faithful.

If we can adequately place ourselves in Job's position, would we have remained faithful? Perhaps you know what it is like to suddenly lose one family member or friend. But how does one wrap their mind around losing all family members? Even if we develop one little plantar wart, don't we complain and hobble around at best? But, to be covered in boils—and Job 7:5 mentions his skin was covered in worms—surely, this must have been beyond one's endurance! And then to add insult to injury, Job had to defend himself against his own friends' crushing words (Job 19:2). Yes, Job's soul had become wounded.

Another instance of woundedness mentioned in the Bible is when David speaks to the Lord in Psalm 51:1-17 concerning a broken spirit and a broken, contrite heart. In Psalm 147:3, David again told us, "He heals the brokenhearted and binds up their wounds." When we consider David's life as an exile, hiding and running from King Saul, in addition to his sins of murder and cohabiting with Bathsheba, Uriah's wife, while Uriah was away at war, we see plenty of trauma and sin creating a vast amount of woundedness.

Six dilemmas, at least, can manifest themselves through the dome of woundedness. First, woundedness can frequently continue to subliminally remind us that we are just pitiful creatures, not good enough for anything, much less to carry the name of Jesus in any fashion or form. After all, with our sins of yesterday, we have brought shame upon the name of Jesus. Our self-worth and confidence in Christ can be trampled under the enemy's ruthless feet.

Second, oozing, gaping soul wounds can also create various types of chronic illnesses and serious diseases such as cancer, to name one. Festering strongholds of woundedness continue building in strength. "The Deadly Consequences of Unforgiveness," a CBN News article based on the findings of Dr. Michael Barry, reported that 61 percent of cancer patients have forgiveness issues in which they have taken offense believing someone or some situation wronged them! That is an astonishing connection! Thus, some physicians have initiated "forgiveness therapy" as an important element in the treatment for cancer.

Third, soul wounds may interfere with us recognizing the need to forgive the one who brought trauma into our lives.

Fourth, the wounds can block or hamper our understanding, discernment, and growth in the Lord; squelch His Word within our spirit; and impede the effectiveness of even sincere prayers.

Fifth, woundedness may undermine and cripple us enough to capture us, then take us backward into repeatedly repeating the same type of sin. Like a yoyo, we work hard at doing what's right. When temptation comes our way, we to swing right back to the starting point again and again. It's as if our spirit and soul have been incarcerated, locked up in a mighty stronghold.

Furthermore, issues of fear, anger, and resentment can be created as it did with Cain in Genesis 4:1-16, causing us to lash out, even in bitter violence. Holding offense is dangerous.

And, the list could continue at great length. Do you have struggles that just will not vanish regardless of what you have tried to do? Perhaps you need healing in your soul of grievous woundedness.

When first becoming acquainted with Katie Souza and Expected End Ministries, she was presenting a message about soul wounds and how those wounds affect our daily lives. Often, we do not realize our physical ailments and bad attitudes can be attributed to difficulties in the spiritual realm.

Souza presented what was a unique and powerful interpretation of God's Word about woundedness. Doesn't God's forgiveness settle all our sin issues? According to Katie, sin is two-fold—it effects our spirit as well as our soul. Katie explained the consequences of woundedness and the soul's need for healing because of its propensity to stockpile perceived injustices. One could say it's somewhat like a packrat; after first stealing and then stowing away a great deal of our personal stuff, it turns and gnaws at every nerve and fiber of our being!

After learning to apply the glory light of heaven in the following manner to my aching heart, to the woundedness within me, it created fabulous freedom. So then how does the soul receive healing? This glory light, of course, is Jesus Christ. And God's power to do whatever He sends His Word to do is *dunamis* power. *Dunamis* is defined from the Greek Lexicon (dictionary) as "moral power and excellence of soul," "an inherent power," "power residing in a thing by virtue of its nature." God, through His [*dunamis*] power, raised Jesus Christ from the grave (Ephesians 1:19-20).

To explain further, a couple of situations are shared below to demonstrate how the application of the glory light of heaven has brought healing to my life. It will bring healing to you as well. In my desire to be clean, pure, and whole before the Lord, I would ask Him to show me any hidden sin, wound, or fault in me that was impeding my walk with Him. The Lord would indeed oblige my request! Again, we must participate by asking. As we come close to God, he comes close to us, (James 4:7-8). Almost always, an awkward incident, usually from my youthful days, would immediately come to mind. It's astonishing at how little ordinary things of life—things that are hardly thought of as sin and committed from the innocence of childhood or those teenage years—do indeed hinder our advancement in Christ and throw us off course! Even if we're only one degree off, we may never reach our intended destination.

You would think that seemingly small unforgiven sin, little stuff, would just evaporate over time and God would forget, pay no attention to it, or not even notice at all. Not true! Regardless of what it is, how old it is, whether we consider it petty or quite significant, or whether we consider ourselves as innocent, sin is sin and must be dealt with according to God's requirements, not by man's logic. If our sin could be managed by our rationale, we would not have needed a Savior. Jesus Christ's living exemplification of holiness, His earthly suffering, and shame on the cross would have totally been in vain.

Among the first situations, a serious matter held up to the light of Jesus Christ, had taken place about sixty years after the fact from the days of elementary school. Briefly, I'll explain. An older teenage acquaintance came along with his parents one beautiful sunny afternoon to visit my family. We lived in a small rural area on a large farm. It was one of those sweet delightful days when a nice drive in the country awakened the senses and freshened the soul. While our parents went inside for some iced tea and more comfortable seating, we continued to hangout in the beauty of the warm sunny day just doing kid stuff. We especially enjoyed the swing set regardless of how small. The bars were still great for swinging and dangling topsy-turvy. Then, horror struck! Being caught totally by surprise, this trusted acquaintance's sudden evil intentions held me in terror! He abruptly grabbed both my hands and flung me up against the wall of our near-by garage. In shock and

disbelief, feeling trapped and grossly overpowered, I succumbed to a gush of tears as my eight-year-old body went as limp as yesterday's droopy dandelions. Thankfully, as he noticed the flood of unrelenting tears, he released me. Running to the house as fast as my young legs could carry me, angrily and defiantly, I yelled back at him, sobbing, "I'm going to tell on you!" Even though, I was not physically harmed, my soul was scared with betrayal. Part of me wanted revenge! Offense and unforgiveness had set themselves on a pathway of destruction within my being.

Later, years later, when I saw him with his wife, those old emotions to "tell on him," rose up, still fresh. "Imagine what his wife would do if she knew about his darkness," I thought with contempt. But short of giving dirty looks, I was too shy to say anything. Instead I seethed in silence.

After that scene had replayed in my mind, I followed an outline of action taught by Katie Souza. Even though innocent from this atrocity, I asked the Lord to take the scrub brush of the blood of Jesus and scour away any sin from that incident including my sense of offense and desire for revenge. You see, my response to the sin imposed upon me, caused me to sin, too. Even though my reaction was well within the boundaries of what we would say is normal, holding the offense was the problem. Then I praised the Lord for as long as I wholeheartedly felt praise for His cleansing and for His forgiveness. Next, I asked the Lord to use His *dunamis* power, which is embodied within His glory light, to heal the woundedness within my soul. The Lord removed from my soul the effects of what sin had engaged in me. Finally, I asked the Lord to produce in me excellence of soul (3 John 1:2 KJV). Following these moments there was more sincere praise and thanksgiving. It was completed. Sin and woundedness from this issue were healed.

Shortly after this experience, my path crossed again with this man, now in his senior years, along with all his family members. Compassion was all I felt for him and his family. The desire for revenge, wanting to expose his darkness, was gone. The grief from broken trust had also vanished! Praise God from whom all blessings flow! I had been set free! We can be assured that our wounds have been healed simply by our positive response to new circumstances involving old confrontations.

Being set free from woundedness doesn't mean the other person and I should be best of friends. No, not at all. But I could be sincere and friendly. A discerning distance is wise. I had indeed forgiven him and had no remaining revenge in me. Furthermore, I believe he most likely would have liked to have asked my forgiveness for that unpleasant moment in history but just did not have the courage or possibly no opportunity. Either way, it matters not.

Incidentally, a short time ago after mediating upon God's goodness, I asked the Lord, "Why did this man, just a young teen at the time, release me without physical harm?" The Lord revealed an awesome truth. "There was just enough of the Holy Spirit within him to act with compassion to the distress he had created." Even though he apparently had serious issues, he also knew about Jesus. Furthermore, he had a praying mother.

Another illustration follows to demonstrate how even our unknown sin and woundedness can encumber the work God wants to do within us. The spiny tentacles of arrogance do not go unnoticed!

Toward the close of a delightful day spent with my childhood best friend and classmate, Joanie (not her real name) and I were holed up in her room discussing boys. It just so happened that Joanie's somewhat younger brother also had a friend, Mike (not his real name), spending the day with him. It was Mike that we girls were appraising. More honestly, we were deliberately and scathingly berating him behind his back. "I didn't like the way he..." "She didn't care for the way he..." "He was such a..." "Why did he act so...?" You get the picture. Our banter continued. A scandalous conversation it was—until both boys abruptly popped out from Joanie's closet, proudly exclaiming, "We heard every word!" They raptly bombarded us girls with what they thought of us! Well! In disgust, we returned the fire, unloading on them in the most arrogant of fashion. "Eavesdropping! How could you betray us like this?" . . . and so on. It's a wonder we all remained friends.

Just ordinary teenage entanglements, right? Maybe so. I mean, what teenage girl or boy has not talked about the other in some derogatory manner? However, it had unknowingly crippled my soul, my prayer life, until the Lord brought me to repentance. And, yes, as an older adult, I had to humble myself and, feeling a bit embarrassed,

ask Mike for forgiveness as well. (He readily forgave and stated he didn't even remember the incident.)

I followed the same format as mentioned earlier asking the Lord to cleanse my soul with the scrub brush of the blood of Jesus and use His *dunamis* power to heal the woundedness within bringing to me excellence of soul as well as including heartfelt sincere praise and adoration to the Lord. I was amazed at how light and fresh I felt on the inside of my being. It was a source of elation. God was doing a new thing in me. He sees every defiling device and desires to cleanse us from the devil's clutches. God wants nothing to hinder the power of our prayer life because it is directly related to our relationship with Him. He desires to instill in us the foundation of a pure heart—our future depends upon it because sin gives our adversary an open door to attack us.

The glory light of heaven has such immense power! As we participate, act, and involve ourselves in God's healing process, new abundant life of *grace* permeates those old wounds of distress and sorrow causing them to vanish.

There were other happenings in my soul that needed healing as well. God reminded me that I had not truly forgiven my first husband (now deceased) for his betrayal of faithfulness to the ideals of our marriage relationship. Validation for shame I had so unwittingly participated in yesteryears ago was blamed, in part, on him. This also opened the door for further deception. Hebrew 12:15 cautions us, "See to it that no one falls short of the grace of God and that no bitter root grows up to cause trouble and defile many." Though it was not consciously recognized, a bitter root, resentment, within me had flourished and grown into great tree. Sadly, our sins effect those around us, especially those closest to us. Like a long line of dominoes, one fall can create a fall for all. Wickedness stops at nothing except the power within the Word of God! "For the word of God is alive and powerful. It is sharper than the sharpest two-edged sword, cutting between soul and spirit, between joint and marrow. It exposes our innermost thoughts and desires" (Hebrews 4:12 NLT). Remember, Jesus, during His days of temptation, defeated Satan by stating, "It is written..." (Matthew 4:4-6). Due to the thorough healing power of the Glory Light of heaven, let us remember we are covered by *grace.* Jesus replaces our woundedness with excellence of soul.

A multitude of other examples could be shared, but the point is this: As our souls undergo and continue to undergo the process of heaven's demolition, removing the old self and building renewed life through the glory light of Heaven, we are set free—free like a butterfly released at long last to radiate its lustrous iridescence as it unfolds its wings in freedom from its barred confines! One step at a time, as each deposit of sin and each layer of pain is removed from our soul, God is proceeding right along with His blueprints of restoration.

Healing our woundedness brings strength, boldness, clearer understanding, better communication, obedience, and a knowing of the depth and width and height and length of God's love like it was never experienced before. More excellence of abiding in Christ will be relished. We will bask in the presence of Jesus completed by His love and grace. We will know that Jesus Christ is enough. His grace fills us with everything as we raise our hands to honor Him. In the process we relinquish everything our hands hold on to, bringing us into excellence of abiding. God's glorious grace, His unmerited and undeserved favor will continually be infused into our souls. God is in the process of designing us with a soul of excellence. What God does for one of His children, He will do for all, for He is no respecter of persons.

In Exchange

*W*E EACH, ARE COVERED by God's grace as we come to Him individually. We exchange within our spirit every sin and brokenness with the robe of Christ's righteousness. The blood of Jesus has cleansed and made us whole. Believe it, accept it in the same manner your salvation was received—by faith. When the enemy tries to defeat us, we can simply decree, "God says there is therefore now, no condemnation to those in Christ Jesus who walk not after the flesh, but after the [Holy] Spirit" (Romans 8:1 HCSB). Or declare Colossians 1:13: "For He has rescued me out of the dominion of darkness and has brought me into the kingdom of the Son He loves."

The very thing most feared—exposure of shame—is the springboard from which fresh new life appears. Much like a gutted and razed building, the spirit within from the foundation upward is rebuilt, renovated, and re-established for His glorious purposes and covered by His grace.

God, in His infinite understanding of mankind, does not expect us to be perfect in every manner. He does, however, expect us to be righteous. How can this be? Remember Abraham in the old testament? He believed God, the Eternal God, to be the one true God while everyone else in his day believed in many gods. Because of his trust in God, he acted and followed God's directions to leave his home in Haran and "head to a land that I will show you" (Genesis 12:1). Again, however much later, Abraham followed God's directions to give Isaac, Sarah and his miracle son, as a sacrifice (Genesis 22). Romans 4:3 tells us it was credited to him as righteousness. Abraham had great faith and trust in God as well as keen hearing and understanding of what God's directions were, yet he wasn't perfect. God works through people despite our shortcomings, and in some cases because of them. In our weaknesses God's strength is poured out (2 Corinthians 12:9).

Two examples illustrate how Abram, later named Abraham, was as human as you and I—not exactly perfect. One, it was with an impatient heart that he listened to Sarah when the waiting for God's promised child seemed too impossible in their old age. Perhaps, they reasoned, God meant for Sarah's Egyptian maid to be the surrogate mother of Abraham's child, an acceptable practice in that day and age. And so, Ishmael was born, but his birth caused much discord between Sarah and her maid, Hagar. However, about thirteen years later when Abraham was one hundred years old, Isaac was born! Isaac was the covenant son God had promised. Hagar and Ishmael were sent away. Surely, Isaac was the apple of his daddy's eye and the joy of his mother's heart. God's promise had been fulfilled (Genesis 21:1-5).

Another time, again before God had named Abram, Abraham, out of fear, he asked Sarah to pretend to be his sister as they passed through the country of Egypt—not once but twice! (Abraham was not exactly lying because Sarah was indeed his half-sister. They shared the same father but had different mothers. In this era, marrying a relative was not a problem but preferred.) He feared they would see Sarah's great beauty, have him killed, and keep Sarah for their own. This not only created more difficulties for Abraham, but also for Pharaoh the Egyptian king and again with Abimelech, King of Gerar. And still, Abraham is counted as righteous.

"For I know the plans I have for you," declares the Lord, "plans to prosper you and not to harm you, plans to give you hope and a future. Then you will call on me and come and pray to me, and I will listen to you. You will seek me and find me when you seek me with all your heart" (Jerimiah 29:11-13).

"For we are His creation, created in Christ Jesus for good works, which God prepared ahead of time so that we should walk in them" (Ephesians 2:10 HCSB).

Our Lord loves us with a love so profound that we can hardly fathom the scope of it.

Because of this love He continually sends His encouragement telling us to look ahead toward our future not our past. Hallelujah!

> *"...The Lord appeared to us in the past, saying:*
> *'I have loved you with an everlasting love;*
> *I have drawn you with unfailing kindness.*
> *I will build you up again, and you,*
> *Will be rebuilt.'*
> *Again, you will take up your timbrels*
> *And go out to dance with the joyful...*
> *Come, let us go up to Zion,*
> *To the Lord our God."*
>
> *-Jeremiah 31:1-6*

GRACE EBBS IN

Inevitably grief, pain, and shame arrive,
Hiding themselves deeply in the recesses of the soul,
Feigning nonexistence.

They lay sleepily
In quiet tentacles of growth
Yet in want of freedom.

In fear, a guarded lonely tear escapes,
Recognizing, holding back,
Testing, discerning, detecting.

Privately, the woundedness
Lashes out,
Releasing regret, anguish, fear.

Love and *grace* ebb in,
Slowly replacing the sting of shame.
God's *grace* begins its transformation.

Intercession, acceptance, wisdom enter.
Self exposed to self,
Peace, long awaited, graces the surface.

Roots of transformation
Hunger for more of God's marvelous *grace*.
Gently, humble healing arrives within the soul.

New life blossoms,
Fed internally through God's glorious *grace*,
And welcomes wholeness.

by MaB

GRACE RELEASED

*I*S IT POSSIBLE TO portray the hushed passion of being covered by *grace* into an illustrious illustration? For me, when I ponder upon all that the Lord continues to devise within my heart and spirit, the awesomeness and wonder of God's love goes far beyond the spoken word into the essence of profound divine, such as in touching or being swallowed up within the glory of a stunning sun burst after the rain. A new love or being enfolded with golden threads may express the architecture of the holiness found in *grace*. And, how about the peace of God that passes all earthly understanding? Perhaps you can relate to some of these, or possibly, you recall other especially personal and meaningful circumstances.

In a sense being *covered by grace* may be akin to:

That one stunning sunset, incredibly spectacular. You stopped what you were doing, being adrift in awe and wonder. Maybe you were driving down a familiar roadway or boating out on a lake or walking along a quiet country path when you took notice. That one sunset when all time stood still as you gazed, spellbound in its splendor—being too sacred to fully absorb its harmonizing hues of glorious yellows and orange, whispers of magenta and indigo on an enormous canvas of royal blue. That sunset seemed to illuminate the priceless signature of God, "My peace, my love, as a gift, I give to you my child." As you held your eyes attentive attempting to memorize detail upon detail of His masterpiece, the Lord's presence was so obviously near. It caused you to overflow with joyous peace and confidence—like a tiny taste of

heaven's grandeur. The glory of that sunset radiated with the unfailing awe of forgiveness and God's *grace*!

That new-found love. You found sentiments of love and joy from a depth you didn't realize existed until this very moment. You felt it while holding your newborn infant or grandbaby. Perhaps you felt mesmerized by the miracle of life? Did your heart swell up in such wonderment that it rolled up in awe like glistening pearls slipping down your cheek in the innocence of mystery? The glory of this incredible loving moment radiates with the awe found in God's *grace* as well.

That golden thread. Do you relish lounging and resting snuggly blanketed beneath the sensation of cozy luxury, with your toes burrowing into the caressing warmth of Sherpa softness? It's like a golden thread wrapping and encapsulating you into a cocoon of completeness, relaxing quiet, and peace. That quiet adornment of *grace*, peace and rest also equates to the emotional state found in God's *grace*.

That calming tranquil flow. Perhaps finding the simplicity in receiving *grace* is as simple as the tranquil flow within your mind after holding your breath ten seconds in preparation for a stressful situation. Remember the exuding calm as you slowly exhaled? That calm equates to receiving God's *grace* also.

Accepting and receiving God's *grace* into your spirit is akin to the physical sense of peace, love, joy, awe and wonderment as painted above. The soul feels such a rush of peace and heavenly love that the harassment of doubt, shame, sorrow, humiliation, relentless self-condemnation, and remorse are completely covered and annihilated within God's *grace*.

Ah, the fabulous feel of the Lord's inviting touch, allows us to feel washed, pure and spotless, by the scrub brush of the blood of Jesus! It is unspeakably incredible!

We are totally and eternally forgiven as we surrender, exchanging our transgressions for the incredible freedom from the ball and chain of sin and shame. As we allow the Lord to complete His work in us, within our memories, He will continue to heal our woundedness and cause our soul to prosper. We see the crippling sting of sin dissolve (3 John 1:2).

CHANGING GEARS

"For God did not give us a spirit of timidity or cowardice or fear,
but [He has given us a spirit] of power and of love and of sound
judgment and personal discipline [abilities that result in a calm,
well-balanced mind and self-control]" 2 Timothy 1:7 AMP

$\mathcal{T}$HROUGHOUT *COVERED BY GRACE* we have looked at spiritual struggles that follow devastation in our lives due to our own sad choices. It is that very sense of failure that grips ahold of us with fingers of steel and will not let go until we change gears, change our thinking.

We know everyone else has failures of one sort or another, whether significant or insignificant—just not us. Of course, to us, our personal failure feels more like a massive catastrophe! Usually, our disappointment can be managed well enough as long as our peers are not privy to that knowledge. Whether we want to admit it or not, their judgements do matter. To begin with, it can be immensely humbling, humiliating, and demeaning, which in turn fills us with condemnation, remorse and shame! It seems we have the impression that success is all that matters. Furthermore, it seems to be acceptable in society and generally in life that we must maintain that "A+" on the rubric scale of opinions.

Speaker and Clinical Psychologist, Dr. Henry Cloud, who has also authored several books candidly shared from *The Power of the Other*. Here, he explains his own anguish with failure and feeling like a loathsome loser during a dark period in his business: "The '*fangs*' of

the beast that was slaying me were feelings of judgment, failure, guilt, shame, and condemnation for missing the standard against which I was judging myself… winners don't blow it this badly." These were his words, but also my identical feelings toward my own personal failures. What released Dr. Cloud from the "fangs," as he called the stronghold held against him, was something quite simple. Freedom came when one of his business friends stated, "We've all been there." No judgement. No condemnation.

From my view, I see comradery as being especially important for success. The freedom to follow the Lord's direction for writing Covered by *Grace* came from beyond the vision of obedience, even as important as that is. It came slowly but surely as I acted upon one prompting and then another to risk confiding in a trusted friend about my involvement with a shameful sin of yesteryears. More importantly, additional freedom came when that friend did not condemn me but maintained our friendship. In turn, that gave me the courage to share again when prompted by the Lord and then again with the same results of forgiveness and friendship. Speaking aloud—that is confessing the sin as well as confessing God's Word as mentioned throughout *Covered by Grace*—concerning the bondage sin had puts us in, gradually resulted in freedom from that shadowy stain of shame and guilt-ridden remorse.

Looking back, historically, we discover that numerous individuals are credited as being successful only because of their failures. In secular society back through recent centuries as well as through God's servants from over two thousand years ago, we see failure, then great success from the same individuals, such as with King David, King Saul, Solomon, apostle Peter, and apostle Paul as discussed in previous chapters. Their personal implosions caused them to change their thinking and to reassess their goals, especially as followers of God Almighty. I'm confident that if you search the Internet for "successful people who first failed," you would be rewarded with a vast and diverse collection of anecdotes.

Failing in and of itself can be an incredibly eye-opening wealth of education and give us tremendous insight *if* we carefully re-examine our situation. We'll find our weak link, make changes, and turn it for personal growth as well as maturing in our Christian walk as we place our pride at the feet of Jesus Christ. In Proverbs 3:5, we find the Lord tells us "not to lean upon our own understanding, but trust in the Lord with all our heart." While this is true, from the get-go, it is far better to be obedient to God's Word and forego suffering the penalties of sin.

It is Christ, through the Holy Spirit, who strengthens us and encourages us to continue abiding in Him. From the beginning, you may have known all the truths mentioned above, but have you allowed the Holy Spirit to be your counselor and to internalize the truth within your spirit? Have you applied them to your specific situation through the wisdom and strength of the Lord? If not, it may be helpful for you to decree and declare this scripture aloud: *"I can do everything through Christ who strengthens me"* (Philippians 4:13 ESV).

Recovering from condemnation and shame is not magical, like, "just say the magic words and presto we're all better." Some serious soul searching is needed, and then there is the searching to develop a proper perspective in Christ. Ordering our words according to the Word of God is extremely powerful.

Shame and guilt can be powerful tools for dismantling our walk with the Lord, but let us also remember that these very same issues can become the product of promotion. A few years ago, our Executive pastor at Trinity Lighthouse in Denison, TX, Gwen England, stated in one of her Wednesday evening messages (I paraphrase) that God uses the garbage or rubbish of our individual lives as fertilizer, just like a gardener uses manure to fertilize and sustain lush picturesque foliage. The rains come watering and penetrating the nutrients into the roots of our lives in Christ. What began as a stench transforms us into richness of growth and beauty. God has a way of working it into the soil of our spirit and soul, in turn causing us to thrive and to blossom. He envelopes us into the sweet fragrance of His love and grace.

How is it that one continues to be preoccupied with remorse and grief from their shame and guilt to the point of being *haunted* daily by the memory yet know without a shadow of doubt that their sins against God and others are forgiven?

After hearing Dr. Cloud speak at a Ladies' Conference in Fort Worth, TX, concerning the stronghold of defeat, it all finally made sense. He explained (again, I paraphrase) that when we perceive ourselves to be in a stressful and negative state of being, perhaps due to a colossal and humiliating mistake, our mind, the spirit, and the

soul are all spiraling downward. The brain releases toxic thoughts of self-condemnation. It continues to harass us, thus taking us deeper and deeper into a depression. But, if we have a trusted friend or counselor whom we hold in high esteem who will honestly listen to our story of failure and then reply, "We've all made mistakes, we've all sinned," and possibly in addition share a personal incident. It can destroy the grip of fear linked to the exposure. The sharing process can loosen some of our woundedness. We begin to think rationally again. The depression lifts. We can once again make good decisions and carry on with the work at hand.

At the same time, some people say, "The harassment will stop when you have forgiven yourself for personal errors including hauntingly despicable sins." I ask you, with what strength, authority, or power do I eradicate my own sin? Even though I can say, "I forgive me, and I'm sorry." the words are empty. They are powerless to erase the memories and the self-condemnation.

An example set by Apostle Paul in 1 Timothy 1:12-17 straight forwardly admits the fact that he considers himself the chief of sinners. His attitude was matter-of-fact, accepting the past (his murderous attempt to annihilate the Christians) as being a done deal. He seemingly focused on what he knew God was directing him to do. Indeed, the love and forgiveness of our Lord extends far beyond our capability of understanding. In another scripture, Paul states that he doesn't look to the past but to the future (Philippians 3:13-15). In addition, Paul seemed to have no fear of other people's opinions. He dared anyone, except Christ, to judge him (1 Corinthians 4:2-5). His forgiveness and cleansing came from the Lord alone. Did he forgive himself? I believe apostle Paul was so assuredly and confidently full of Jesus Christ there was no place for self or self-condemnation. He was bold and strong willed, held strong beliefs, and had a "get 'er done" mentality. He had enough of self and his sinful murderous deeds as a Pharisee. He accepted Jesus Christ as the Son of God, a 180 degree turn in his belief system, through the experience of being physically blinded by the Lord for three days while on his way to Damascus; a powerful change had taken place. At this point, his name was still Saul. Not only had God changed his thinking, He also changed his name to Paul! Through being physically blind, he could finally see spiritual truth, strength, and the power of the Almighty God! He had finally met, firsthand, the Lord of Lords, to whom he could only surrender. Saul, now Paul, was a changed man by God's own hand.

In another instance within the Lord's prayer (Matthew 6:9-13), we ask the Lord to forgive us in the same manner as we have forgiven those who have sinned against us. I do not see that we are asked to forgive ourselves. For me, I knew the sins I had committed quite well; fear, regret, and the shame of those sins had me in a vice grip. I absolutely had no power to release myself from that stronghold. Our adversary, the accuser of the brethren, will relentlessly pick our bones clean with one accusation after another like a vulture. He has no mercy. It is the *Word* that sets us free from the power of darkness (Colossians 1:13). We can, however, add strength to our battle plans through utilizing the power of our testimony (Revelations 12:11). In other words, we can decree and declare God's Word over ourselves. His Word does not return void. It goes out to accomplish all that God has purposed for it to do (Isaiah 55:11).

Of course, in our attempt to change, several things are going on emotionally and spiritually. In my experience, unlike apostle Paul, clearly my first major issue was fear. Fear of all the "what-ifs." Fear of condemnation. Fear of exposure. Fear of judgment. I was paralyzed with fear. Since God is not the author of fear, we know without a doubt that the accuser, Satan, is working to condemn us, weakening the word of our testimony, holding us captive in sorrowful deception, and in turn preventing us from joyfully serving the Lord.

Consequently, to make a change, first off, let us search deep within and ask, have we come face to face with absolute truth of the matter? Have we admitted to ourselves the reality of the facts? Pay close attention to the attitude from which we answer. Do we make excuses and place the blame for sin on others? Do we whine and complain? Do we attempt to justify our actions? On the other hand, do we simply expose the truth with unencumbered admission, like the apostle Paul, "Yes, I sinned. Yes, I committed this abominable thing." From the beginning of our honest admission of guilt and asking the Lord to cleanse and heal our wounds, God can begin His cleansing reconstruction within us. Sometimes healing comes in small doses, like a gentle breeze such as when we visit one-on-one with a trusted

confidant, counselor, and/or prayer warrior. Other times, healing may come like a mighty wind, full of fervor, strong and emboldened.

Or perhaps another option, exposing the struggle in black and white (such as with journaling), would be more suitable for healing. Writing and study can bring remarkable healing. Yet I remember attending a ladies' Christian retreat, obviously cringing in fear when it was advised that we ladies make a list, privately, of all our sins and regrets. Our God fearing gentle leader had been sharing snippets of her own wretched past before she became a child of God and how writing could release the stinging tentacles of sin. Now at this point, she seemed to be looking, seeing straight through me, as I ardently recoiled. Fear was stalwartly in control. I considered my past sin as too evil to even remember, let alone reveal even privately on paper, with only my eyes to see in the light of day. I could not risk spotlighting sin, my failure—the disgrace so deeply dark.

Possibly, you feel the same way about an immense failure. However, God ministers to us through the Holy Spirit, who is forever kind, loving, and gentle. He reaches down into the core of our need with His unique quiet strength and soothing tenderness. While the Lord does not condone or wink at our sin, He never ridicules or blames. He never holds us in contempt for our lack of perfection. The Lord says, "Come close, my dear one. Allow me to demonstrate the length, depth, height, and width of My love."

Again, as we expose the accuser, his attacks begin to weaken, especially as we pray together, binding his maligning spiritual iron grip and releasing God's glory light of healing, the light of Jesus Christ, within us. As we depend upon the Lord's touch, the clutch of strongholds is loosened off our back, loosened out of our mentality, and cleaned out of our emotions, liberating us to be who God has called us to be.

Tony Evans, pastor of Oak Cliff Bible Fellowship, as well as president of Urban Alternatives, and author of numerous best sellers, a favored conference, television, and radio speaker, has stated "God is after one thing—a change of heart and character in each of us. God can restore us, redeem us, heal us, and even promote us *if* we will say, "Search me, God, and know my heart; test me and know my anxious thoughts. See if there is any offensive way in me and, lead me in the way everlasting" (Psalm 139:23-24).

Our enemy, the adversary, indeed wants to distract, discourage, deflate, defeat, and devalue us with every breath we take. He is the author of lies, confusion, death to dreams and our purpose. But God's Word says we can do all things through Christ Jesus who strengthens us. Do not despair! Our life in Christ continues. Our Lord waits for us to take hold of His truth and move forward in His purposes.

All scripture is powerful, but this is one you may want to have ready and on call so to decree and declare aloud during desperate moments: *"God has pulled us [me] out of the power of darkness and into His most marvelous and glorious light"* (Colossians 1:13)! Through repentance and our trust in God's love, His Word, and His forgiveness, condemnation, remorse, shame, and the misery of self-pity, have no hold on us!

Recalling an occasion when I believed I had denied Christ Jesus helps illustrate the profound power of the above scripture. This scenario begins as I was becoming acquainted with a new friend, Andrew (not his real name), who was an assigned seat partner while on an international flight to visit family members. While stowing my carryon luggage, I gained a trace of insight regarding his faith as I overheard his polite but short conversation with the stewardess. So, in concert with the motions of settling in and buckling up, I jubilantly confirmed that he was of the Jewish faith. He in turn asked about my stance on religion. I had begun joyfully voicing, "Oh, I love…" and was about to say, "Jesus," when, in a brief nanosecond, my mind heard the words, "Remember what the leader from your recent retreat said? Just be casual." So I interrupted my train of thought to say, "I love . . . the Lord." Amiable conversation continued for the duration of the nine-hour flight. In addition, once on the ground, he, like an angel, guided me through the airport to catch my next connection even though I believe he may have missed his. Then came the time to exchange parting farewells.

Several weeks later, after returning home, I was suddenly inundated with powerful and remorseful regret. I felt and strongly believed that I had betrayed Jesus because I had not answered Andrew with the fact that I loved Jesus as I had intended. I had substituted, "Lord" which could mean a lot of things. Nothing would dismiss the torturously fierce accusations of betrayal! I felt alienated from the Lord. I cried buckets of tears, I prayed, I begged the Lord to forgive me, and I identified with

the crushing bitter defeat apostle Peter must have experienced when he had denied Christ three times (Mark 14:66-72). I attempted to sing praises. I read God's Word. I heard prophesy that yesterday is gone, look only to today, continue in God's path; in addition, I confessed my sin to various individuals as well as to our Bible study group. Others prayed for me. All these righteous actions were somewhat helpful, but nothing removed the ongoing harassment! I was seriously beside myself with anguish! There was absolutely no consolation! None!

Then one evening, through torrents of tears, I was reading aloud scriptures about who I am in Christ. Immediately, within a blink of an eye, upon reciting Colossians 1:13 in desperation, a spirit of overwhelming peace engulfed me completely. *All* menacing strongholds of accusations and harassment had vanished instantly! It was like a refreshing new sunny day after a sweet spring rain. God's Word had purposefully pulled me out and away from the power of darkness! The amazing power held in God's Word is phenomenal! God's Word is indeed alive and active. Hallelujah!

So ultimately, to reach beyond the stronghold of guilt, the shame, the remorse, and the grieving, it's not about forgiving oneself. It's about speaking the life of God's Word into our being and our situation. Numerous spiritual giants in the ministry of God's Word teach us that we cannot depend upon our emotions or feelings to shed truth upon any subject; thus, we must rely wholly on the Word, whether or not we feel forgiven and clean. We are forgiven, and we are clean because the Word says so. We believe it the same way we believe that Jesus has saved us into salvation. "If we confess with our lips that Jesus is Lord and believe in our hearts that God has raised Jesus Christ from the dead, we are saved" (Romans 10:9). Thus, when we feel condemned again and again, acknowledge and confess with our lips that we are forgiven and made whole. Romans 8:1-2 confirms, "Therefore, there is now no condemnation for those who are in Christ Jesus, because through Christ Jesus the law of the Spirit who gives life has set you [me] free from the law of sin and death." Furthermore, let us remember the prayer of, 3 John 1:2, from the New American Standard Bible, as it encourages, "Beloved, I pray that in all respects you may prosper and be in good health [mentally, spiritually, physically, (author's understanding)], just as your soul prospers." I did not need to spend thirty-five years wandering in the desert of shame and fear. But I had allowed the shame to place me in fearful bondage from which I required the power of God's Word to release me.

We remember that our struggle is not against flesh and blood, but against the rulers and authorities, powers, and spiritual forces of evil in the heavenly realms (Ephesians 6:12). It is these spiritual forces of evil, Satan and his underlings, that continue to lie, accuse, and remind us of our past. Or it may be other people who have their own issues defeating them; thus, they keep their eyes on your past. We beat their haranguing message down by speaking the Word, "It is written..., I have been redeemed by the blood of Jesus Christ and will forever live with Him" (Ephesians 1:7, 1 Peter 1:18-19). "God has not given me a spirit of fear, but of power, love, and a sound mind" (2 Timothy 1:7 KJV).

Repeating again as mentioned throughout *Covered by Grace* freedom comes from speaking, believing, and depending upon the Word of God. John 8:36 (AMP) reassuringly states being infused with all the power of heaven: *"So if the Son makes you free, then you are unquestionably free."* Repeat the scripture until it becomes one with your thinking and one with your spirit.

"May Yahweh (God) bless you and protect you. May Yahweh make His face to shine upon you and be gracious to you. May Yahweh look with favor on you and give you peace. In this way they will pronounce My name over the Israelites [and those adopted into the family of God, the Christians], and I will bless them" (Numbers 6:24-27 HCSB).

In Conclusion

"So, let us come boldly to the throne of our gracious God.
There we will receive his mercy,
and we will find grace to help us
when we need it most"
(Hebrews 4:16 NLV).

"Don't copy the behavior and customs of this world,
but let God transform you
into a new person by changing the way you think.
Then you will learn to know God's will for you,
which is good and pleasing and perfect"
(Romans 12:2 NLV).

"Restore to me the joy of your salvation,
and make me willing to obey you.
Then I will teach your ways to rebels,
and they will return to you"
(Psalm 51:12-13 NLV).

Since we cannot reach for anything new with our hands still full of yesterday's stuff, let us purposely drop the junk in order to freely receive God's *grace* with hands of fresh surrender, stepping forward into His wondrously tailor-made plan. Please know it is the Lord who goes before us and works on our behalf. Look what he reveals to us in Isaiah 61 (author's summary).

The Lord says His spirit is upon us. He has called us to proclaim liberty to the captives; He lavishes us with a crown of beauty instead of ashes. He gives us the oil of joy instead of mourning; He gives us the garment of praise for the spirit of heaviness. He has renamed us oaks of righteousness. He rebuilds and renews the ruins; He restores the devastation. He calls us priests of the Lord and ministers of our God. Instead of shame, we receive a double portion and instead of disgrace, we rejoice in our inheritance. He says that all who see us will know He has blessed us. He has clothed us with garments of salvation and arrayed us in robes of His righteousness!

Our Lord is the gracious loving father welcoming us into His presence and into His arms. Let us go now in victory to run the race He has set before us! Hallelujah!

AND YOU?

WHAT ABOUT YOU? WHAT do you say? Pause from your day's agenda for just a moment. Reflect upon your inner self. Allow the Holy Spirit to gently set His search light within as you ponder the following questions. Perhaps they may probe a little deeper and start you on your own journey of freedom. Feel free to pencil in your thoughts. Thank you, dear Reader, for your transparency as you contemplate gaining liberty from shame and remorse. Your response to your conscientious conclusions may be the bright sparkle you've longed for.

Reach out both of your hands in prayer first thing every morning. Ask the Lord to fill you with a double portion of His *grace* to meet the day's demands victoriously. Then decree and declare that you will joyfully walk the path God has set out for you unencumbered. Praise the Lord from whom all blessings come.

Your Sister in Christ,
Mary Berry

Preface

1. What is crippling your spirit?

2. Please describe your greatest hidden fear.

Introduction, Trouble by the Truckload

1. Christians can be easily entrapped when we...

2. In what way are you rebelling against the Lord?

3. Surrender brings...?

Grace Defined

1. What is meant by, "riches of His *grace?*"

2. How do we receive God's *grace?*

3. Name of few of the numerous benefits of His *grace?* Which ones, if any, are more important to you than another?

Just One Tiny Bite

1. Why was it necessary for Adam and Eve to face temptation?

2. What was Eve's deceit?

3. What can set us on a tumultuous trek?

4. Name at least four things we can do to defeat the enemy.

5. How do you apply the armor of God?

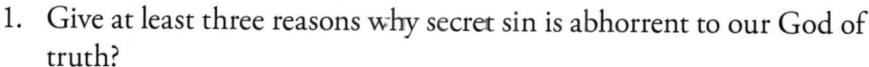

Secrets

1. Give at least three reasons why secret sin is abhorrent to our God of truth?

2. Why does God not leave us in our sinful condition?

Under the Rug

1. From whom do we attempt to hide our sin?

2. What can prevent healing?

Guilty and Undone

1. What actions do you take when seriously tempted with any sin?

2. What are your established relationship boundaries? Are you always mindful of them?

3. Why would the Lord track down His wayward sheep? Are you one of them?

Pursued

1. Where does sin take you?

2. Name at least two important keys to any lasting relationship.

3. Why is "the grass is greener on the other side of the fence" only an illusion?

4. List a couple ways a person can permanently disengage from a sinful relationship.

5. What are three effective means of breaking soul ties?

Your Presence Lord

1. How do you stay in the presence of the Lord daily?

Isn't Knowing Enough?

1. Name at least six mighty servants of God who at first failed.

2. Why isn't knowing right from wrong always enough to keep from sinning?

3. How might you be like King Saul?

4. How does God evaluate your sin?

Slippery Slope

1. Put your motives and attitudes under the microscope. Are you heading down a slippery slope? How do you know?

2. Select at least five different areas to focus your spotlight. What are the indications?

3. Who or what guides your standards for all engagements of life?

The Rescue

1. Who do you say Jesus is?

2. Why did Jesus leave His heavenly throne to come down to us?

Redemption – The Way it Was

1. What was the purpose of the Old Testament sacrifices?

2. How do they relate to Jesus Christ?

Jesus Christ Our Sacrifice

1. How is it that Jesus Christ was a "whipping boy?

2. Would you have been among the crowd, jeering and chanting, "Crucify Him!" repeatedly?

3. Whose sins did Jesus take to the cross?

4. Jesus shed His blood for us eight ways; what are they?

Have You Applied the Blood of Jesus?

1. We can apply the blood of Jesus by....

2. The blood of Jesus has brought deliverance and healing to our souls nine ways; please explain each one.

3. We personalize the scripture by…?

4. What is the correlation between the Last Super, commonly called, communion, and abundant life?

5. Why is it necessary for us to be permeated with the power of the Holy Spirit?

Our Wounded Soul

1. How are soul wounds created?

2. List a few examples of soul wounds.

3. Due to stockpiling our perceived injustices, at least six dilemmas can manifest from a wounded soul. Make a list of these. If you are willing, evaluate them carefully. Do you recognize any of these in your own life?

4. How can you apply the glory light of Jesus to your soul's wounds and receive healing?

Grace Released

1. What does God's *grace* feel like to you?

Changing Gears

1. How has shame, regret, remorse held you back from fulfilling God's purposes in your life?

2. What steps can you take to confidently recover fully from condemnation?

3. What happens in our brain when we make humiliating mistakes?

4. How did the apostle Paul handle the accusations of his past?

5. What steps can you take to move beyond shame and regrets?

6. What are some powerful warfare scriptures you can use to declare and decree freedom from our advisory?

In Conclusion

1. What do the scriptures, Hebrews 4:16, Romans 12:2, and Psalm 12:2 mean to you?

Covered by *Grace*, Other Thoughts...

ACKNOWLEDGEMENTS

*W*HEN WE ACKNOWLEDGE THAT we have been living in a dark, fearful place consumed with doubts and underestimating the power of fear residing in our soul, it is with immense gratitude that we burst through the hardened soil. We are refreshed and joyful due to the Holy Spirit's relentless encouragement. Many times, that encouragement comes from God's servants. You know who you are.

Their forgiveness, their comradery, their acceptance of me even while knowing the truth about dark hidden days of the past has been a powerful elevator lifting me up and out of the miry clay to grow and live in the presence of the Son, Jesus Christ. Thank you for your transparency and friendship. I can only marvel at how the Lord loves His children. Thank you, God Almighty, Lord of Lord's and King of Kings, for your immeasurable love, grace, and mercy.

In addition, I'm eternally grateful for those who gave tremendous encouragement in their own unique manner when I had no strength of my own as it was, as you know, not my idea to write *Covered by Grace*. You kept me moving forward to complete this assignment. I am forever grateful for the accomplishment of being obedient. Honor and recognition belong to you.

To my delightful children, in addition to my brother and sisters and their families who all came along side me with their words of love and support! Each one of them is incredibly wonderful—full of love, forgiveness, compassion, and encouragement. To them I am fully and eternally indebted. You are more precious than rare jewels, silver, and

gold. I love and appreciate you far beyond the most glorious heavenly sunsets, beyond what words can convey. Thank you.

To those friends whom gradually I trusted enough to confide my hidden past and to those whom I believed needed to know before we could be transparent friends. Thank you for your continued friendship, love, and forgiveness. You are a treasure!

To those who lived through these difficult journeys and are directly related to the events within—no animosity is held only forgiveness. Your identities have purposely been omitted for obvious reasons. The Lord has continued to take us on separate paths, paths of righteousness, as we have carried our crosses into the inner chamber of His tabernacle. And I hold deep gratitude for your acts of forgiveness as well.

To Christian fiction authors Francine Rivers with *Redeeming Love,* and Karen Kingsbury with *Where Yesterday Lives,* who penned plot lines filled with dilemmas I identified in myself. I thank you. There are other authors as well that filled my heart with hope and whose creativeness encouraged me to inch closer to the break of day. The Holy Spirit, through your works, met me where my soul was hiding and brought light through varying genres and themes. Thank you!

To two dear friends: Harriett Nix (a retired pastor's wife, Sunday School teacher, and prior editor of a Christian newspaper) and Deena Steen (a counselor, Sunday School teacher and leader of Women of Purpose and Ladies' Leadership Team). Both ladies, beautiful and deeply steeped in the Lord, took time from their busy schedules to prayerfully review and edit *Covered by Grace.* You were ever so gracious with your comments and encouragement. And to a couple of other readers who perused through the manuscript giving me their responses, Thank you ever so much!

To Pastor Brian Ulch, connections pastor, Trinity Lighthouse Church, Denison, Texas. Thank you, more than words can say, for your deeply encouraging words. Thank you as well for lending your expertise through your critique and endorsement of this writing. I greatly appreciate you!

To my pastors, Sunday School teachers, and Kingdom Builders Bible study group who have simply spoken God's word to the masses but specifically into my soul and spirit. I have been listening. You unknowingly have given me courage to continue on the road marked out by the Lord. Thank you ever so much for your faithfulness.

To the Remnant Retreat ladies, Charlene McDonald and Sharon Brooks, who prayed and encouraged me to receive God's direction. Thank you for your keen sensitivity to the Holy Spirit!

To Betts' Ministries and the many individuals within the ministry who have spoken life and courage into my spirit. Thank you. Thank you for your continued prayers on my behalf. Kathy McPherson, thank you for your What's in a Name, Freedom Ministry, and your Dream Interpretations that have caused me to see the truth within my soul. Lee Collum thank you for speaking words from the Holy Spirit that I needed to hear. God has used all of you in a mighty manner!

To Westwood Books Publishing personnel, thank you for your patience and your ever-encouraging words. You have given hope moving this work to accomplishment.

Last but certainly not least, thank you, my friends, the audience and readers of *Covered by Grace*. May the Lord's ministering angels encamp round about you; may the spirit of the Lord bring you peace and a joy unspeakable, along with the light of His truth, healing, and salvation. And may you recognize for yourself the healing *grace* of God.

It is my prayer that the Lord will use *Covered by Grace* in whatever manner He chooses to come alongside you and others who are searching and hungering for freedom from shame. The Lord fills the hungry soul with His goodness and *grace*.

WORKS CITED

A Physician's View of the Crucifixion by Dr. C. Truman Davis, (n.d.). Retrieved June 11, 2018, from http://www1.cbn.com/medical-view-of-the-crucifixion-of-jesus-christ

Becoming A Woman of Excellence, A Bible Study, Cynthia Heald. Navpress, a Ministry of the Navigators. Colorado Springs, CO, 1988.

Cooke, Graham, (2018 August 16). Brilliant TV, *The Mentoring Track, Your Starting Point for Grace* [Video file] Retrieved from https://www.youtube.com/watch?v=_z94tnJRLG8

Deadly Consequences of Unforgiveness by Lori Johnson, (n.d.). Retrieved February 23, 2018, from http://www1.cbn.com/cbnnews/healthscience/2015/June/The-Deadly-Consequences-of-Unforgiveness

Healing the Wounded Soul, 2011, Katie Souza, Expected End Ministries, Phoenix, AZ.

How Many Galaxies are out there? (n.d.). Retrieved October 30, 2017, from https://www.cbsnews.com/news/there-may-be-two-trillion-galaxies-across-the-universe/

How to Apply the Blood of Jesus by Derek Prince, (n.d.). Retrieved October 15, 2017, from https://www.youtube.com/watch?v=RtT6gz3DHTk

Merriam-Webster. (n.d.). Retrieved October 21, 2017, from https://unabridged.merriamwebster.com/subscriber/register/p1?refc=FOOTER_DEF_MWU

The New KJV Testament Greek Lexicon. (n.d.). Retrieved December 30, 2017, from https://www.biblestudytools.com/lexicons/greek/kjv/dunamis.html

The Power of the Blood of Jesus by Andrew Murray (n.d.). Retrieved November 22, 2017 from http://www.worldinvisible.com/library/murray/5f00.0572/5f00.0572.01

Scourging and Crucifixion In Roman Tradition. (n.d.). Retrieved October 16, 2017, from https://www.cbcg.org/scourging-crucifixion.html

Tony Evans. (n.d.) Retrieved November 21, 2017. from https://www.ocbfchurch.org/about-us/dr-tony-evans/

We Must Learn How to Heal the Soul! by Katie Souza. (n.d.). Retrieved December 30, 2017. from https://www.youtube.com/watch?v=t5A9unRhROo

You are welcome to contact author,
Mary Berry,
through the following:

mabteacher@msn.com

CPSIA information can be obtained
at www.ICGtesting.com
Printed in the USA
BVHW071057090820
585894BV00008B/167